THE FRENCH NOVEL

BY

PIERRE MILLE

TRANSLATED FROM THE FRENCH
BY
ELISABETH ABBOTT

PHILADELPHIA & LONDON
J. B. LIPPINCOTT COMPANY
MCMXXX

CONTENTS

THE FRENCH NOVEL

I

PROLOGUE APOLOGETIC

HAD I not had the pleasure of reading "The English Novel"* by Mr. Ford Madox Ford, it never would have occurred to me to write this little book—proof to what extent my English colleague's effort engaged my attention, to what extent, now winning my approval, now causing me to reflect, feel, object, it proved intellectually stimulating to me.

Like my model, or rather like my inspirer—for the plan of this modest work will be wholly different from Mr. Ford's—I have decided to be brief; and to be brief even at the risk of remaining, necessarily, incomplete. My reader will find no erudition in the pages that follow: not even a date, unless the latter should appear, on occasion, absolutely indispensable; not even "literary criticism" in the proper sense of the word! Glorious epochs, illustrious names, a host of authors well deserving of attention, will be passed over in silence; still others will benefit only by mention in a line, in half a line, insufficient, unworthy of them. I think it only honest to warn my reader: I am afraid the real title of these few pages should be: "Idle Thoughts on the French Novel."

*"The English Novel," by Ford Madox Ford, "The One Hour Series," J. B. Lippincott Company.

I might also have called them: "What the French Novel has been, what it is, and what it is going to be." But, apart from the fact that such a title would have been too long, it might, in addition, have seemed pretentious to a degree. Like many people before me I think I know what the French novel has been. But in view of the formidable mass of contemporary writing, it is difficult for me—as for many others—to distinguish really what it is. As for prophesying what it is going to be, that seems to me as idle as speculating on the Yellow Peril, or on the chances the Black Race has of creating an original civilization.

In a brief, but excellent critical biography of Balzac, recently published by M. Pierre Abraham, I have just read the following:

"A glorious year, the year 1831, a year such as one meets but seldom in the history of letters. . . . George Sand and Sandeau publish *Rose et Blanche*; Sand corrects the proofs of *Indiana* . . . Victor Hugo, a year after *Hernani*, brings out *Autumn Leaves* and *Notre-Dame de Paris*. Vigny issues his *Maréchale d'Ancre*. Stendhal does *The Red and the Black*—a work that is soon to founder in forgetfulness."

Today *Rose et Blanche* of George Sand and Sandeau is unknown—except to M. Pierre Abraham whose business it is to know it. *Indiana*, by the same

George Sand, seems to us barely readable: it has passed from the domain of literature into that of literary history—not quite the same thing! I have not read Vigny's *Maréchale d'Ancre*—a sin, perhaps, but a sin I share with many people; whereas, for thirty years, I have never wearied of rereading, and always with the same joy, the same curiosity, the same enthusiasm, *The Red and the Black* and *La Chartreuse de Parme*!

In the face of such precedents, how dare we forecast the future of this or that contemporary novel, or even try to guess the judgment which posterity will pass on it? Moreover, how dare we suggest, pushing temerity still further, that our fiction will take such and such a direction, assume such and such a character? At the most, we may distinguish certain tendencies in it, note (always with proper caution, with the help of this or that example) a few changes it seems to be undergoing, if not in fundamentals, at least in exterior aspect, physiognomy, manner.

Such exterior aspect, physiognomy, manner, may be more or less influenced by material developments in the civilization of the white races: the automobile, the airplane, the moving picture, sports. The new rapidity with which we have learned to perform not only the ordinary acts of life, but its most ambitious activities as well, has taught us to grasp ideas more swiftly and to see more things at one time. In consequence, we demand of our story-tellers greater speed in their manner of telling—less coherence among details perhaps, but a greater multiplicity of them, even at the expense of composition. Or else, on the other hand, we demand a cruder, more synthetic vision of things, something like the impression we receive when driving in an auto at eighty miles an hour—nothing more precise than that! We live more swiftly, we feel more swiftly. And we see and feel different things according as we are travelling on foot, on horseback, by rail, by motor, or by airplane.

But that does not by any means imply that we feel more deeply. Quite the contrary! Our emotions no longer concentrate—we haven't time! Did soul ever feel more deeply than the monk who wrote the *Imitation* without setting foot outside his cell? . . . Whereas the very title—so intelligently significant—of a book by Paul Morand, *Nothing but the Earth*, shows us that in travelling faster and faster, too fast perhaps, with everything appearing to us on one plane, we barely skim the surface of feeling. There is nothing in Morand's book but intelligence, an intelligence which is struggling to get its bearings as best it can in the maze about it. Or else, to put the case inversely, in certain other writers we find a rudimentary vital instinct which enables them to attain an equally rudimentary lyricism, which people have agreed to call "super-realism."

The thing we may distinguish most clearly in contemporary French fiction is the inevitable disappearance of the oratorical style of the Romanticists—a result to which I could very easily be reconciled; whereas (and for this I am inconsolable) the beautiful analytical style of the Eighteenth century, to which Stendhal and Balzac (though they do not pass for great stylists) were so attached, will emerge from the adventure fairly well battered. The analytical style is not swift enough for our time!

But all such changes are superficial. It has been said, à propos of the late war, that even if tactics changed, the principles of strategy remained, as they will always remain, the same. So here as regards fundamentals. The raw material of the novel will always be men and women—consequently love and a society. From the beginning of the world to the end of time a good novel, a great novel, has been and always will be, that novel in which a man or a woman—preferably a man and a woman—appear as definite types, more real than reality.

Moreover, those men and those women must evolve

in a society, and that society must be visible to the eye. Or else the novel, by its influence, must regenerate or create a society.

Great novels will always fall into one or the other of these twin categories.

II

THE ORIGINS OF THE NOVEL

THE *roman* or "novel," it might be said, is as old as literature itself; for, after all, the *Iliad* and the *Odyssey* are novels. It matters little that they be called "epics": the *Iliad* is a novel of martial, the *Odyssey* a novel of maritime, adventure. It matters little, likewise, that these epic romances be written in verse. Prose had scarcely begun to be used, for the public, until after both writing and printing had become general and an author was able to address his individual readers as man to man. Before those discoveries, recitation was the only effective means of reaching a public that could not read. Even recitation depended upon singing (at least upon the chant)— whence the metrical form, which must have been in the beginning an aid to memory, pure and simple. It is much easier to remember a rhymed strophe, particularly when sung, than a bit of prose. But, it will be objected—what of the historians: Herodotus, Thucydides, Livy, Tacitus, and the monk-chroniclers of the Middle Ages? True enough! Works in prose were read aloud —at least the works of the historians. It is extremely probable, however, that readings of this kind were addressed to much smaller audiences (just as history in our day has fewer readers) than the epics, all of these, I repeat, from the *Iliad* to the *Chanson de Roland* and other *chansons de geste, romans*, "novels". Nor was it long before the *chansons de geste* were called "romances"—"romances of chivalry"—that is to say, novels! From such "romances", in fact, *roman*, the French word for novel, has come.

However, it is but honest to add: the true novel, the novel in prose, put in a very early appearance. *Daphnis and Chloe* was in prose. So was *The Golden Ass*. So was *Theagenes and Chariclea*, which Racine read and re-read till he knew it by heart. And not only these—which I mention because everybody knows them, at least by name: there were hundreds of others, a goodly number of them still readable today! Written originally in Greek, they have come down to us only in Low (very low!) Latin translations made as late as the Christian era, and even as late as the Middle Ages, which proves how long interest in them persisted. Some of them I have read. They are sufficiently amusing for me to regret, at times, that one or two of the best were never expurgated *ad usuam puerorum*, and placed in the hands of school children beginning the study of Latin, along with the *De viris* and the *Selecta*. They are almost invariably adventure stories: shipwrecks, magic, pirates, witches, incredible ups-and-downs of fortune and misfortune on the part of youths and maidens well-born. It is amusing to see how sometimes these virgins, who for that matter soon cease to be such, remind us of Cunégonde in *Candide*, but a *Candide* written without imagination and with a very long face.

But were they really so serious? The thought has sometimes occurred to me, in the course of such readings, that this may not always have been the case. It has occurred to me that the irony of the Greek authors may perhaps have been lost in the awkward Latin translations. The medieval translator may not always have grasped the finer slants! Such things have been known to happen even in our day!

The stage on which these adventures evolve embraces, I may add, the whole circuit of the Mediterranean, an evidence of the vast expansion of Greco-Latin civilization in the first centuries after Christ. Everyone, even in France and Spain, had been hearing for centuries of Cyrene, Cappadocia, Egypt, Asia Minor. The people of France and the people of Spain had never seen those lands with their own eyes. They were aware, however, of their existence, and they knew that life went on in them pretty much as it did in their own countries, with enough minor differences to excite curiosity without occasioning bewilderment. Is not that the case, in our own day, with a novel of Paul Morand or Luc Durtain, where the scenes are laid now in the Pacific, now in Siam, now in New York or Hollywood?

And we Frenchmen, in our Middle Ages, and also in prose, had our *Petit Jehan de Saintré* (a love story), not to mention any number of "romances of chivalry" —and *contes*! The *conte* or tale, a popular *genre*, is, quite frankly the written transcription of a story that is "told aloud" (*conté*), as its name indicates.

We cannot, alas, deal with the short story in this essay. I am limited to the novel and must keep within my bounds. And how sorry I am! For one thing, there is something essentially French about the short story. And then, I can make but a bare mention of Guy de Maupassant, who was a story-teller if ever there was one, and sprang from the purest and raciest vein of our ancient tradition. Nor can I devote more than a word here to something that must be apparent to everyone: that Anatole France himself was especially and essentially a short story writer; that his masterpieces beyond all question are, not the *Red Lily* nor even *The Gods Athirst*, profound and keen as those novels are; but short, very short, stories, which, at one time, he could chisel like so many cameos—*The Procurator of Judea*, or the inimitable *Saint-Satyre* in *The Casket of Jewels*. His *Thaïs*, one should remember, was in the beginning a short story barely forty pages long. That it attained the dimensions we now know was the result of a clever and charming ruse on the part of Mme. de Caillavet. That faithful and devoted woman may have had some peculiarities, which an indiscreet biographer of Anatole France has emphasized too much. At any rate she atoned for them by a passionate devotion to her "great man". Mme. de Caillavet wanted Anatole France to appear at his best: she wanted him to write a book which would look the part by having a bulk commensurate with its excellence! She arranged, accordingly, for France to give a reading of the story at her house—if my memory serves, Paul Bourget attended. The auditors had been warned in advance, and at the proper time began exclaiming:

"That is more than a short story, France! You have material there for a novel, a magnificent novel!"

And she:

"You must write it! . . ."

So France wrote it. He wrote it by adding a lot of dialogue to a short story (not that the dialogue is not a wonderful thing, in itself)!

With these tributes safely off my mind I must go back to my subject. I was speaking of our *Petit Jehan de Saintré*, a love story. There were many others like it in the Middle Ages: for that was the age when love was introduced into the novel and into society—love as we know it today.

People have had their fun with the historian Seignobos for having said, in one of those meaty general statements of a paradoxical turn of which he was so fond: "Love is an invention of the Twelfth century . . ." It was Gustave Théry, repeating the apothegm—not Seignobos himself—who wrote *Thirteenth* century (in truth, an unforgivable error!). It was the Twelfth century, let there be no mistake about it; and in saying what he said, Seignobos was only drawing conclusions from theories put forward by very authoritative scholars of his time, by the late Gaston Paris, for example. And he was right, absolutely right! Down to the Middle Ages love was only "Eros"; that is to say, love was sexual desire in men and in women, with the man's conviction of his superiority over the woman, and the woman's conviction of her inferiority to the man, along with a firmly rooted idea that it was a woman's duty to be submissive to her man. So it is, even today, in the Easts, Near and Far.

Feudalism overthrew this conviction: a revolution of the most far-reaching results. For it is only since the institution of the feudal régime that we find the "lord," the "master," and his wife, "the lady," the "mistress," served no longer by slaves, but by men of their own

rank, men of equally noble blood, who were, nevertheless, united to them by bonds of vassalage. It was no
longer a disgrace to serve. And, in fact, everybody
served. You began as a page, you became a squire, and
finally a knight; and you served your "lord" and therefore, at the same time, you served his lady, your "mistress." That is how the word "mistress" came into our
language, and into almost all the languages of the
West, to denote the woman who is not your wife, but
to whom you give yourself and who gives herself to you.

A free gift, be it noted, on the part of the woman!
Her social position remaining theoretically superior,
she remained (at least in theory) the superior of her
lover, equality being reestablished—so far as it was reestablished—only by love, a love that was as great on
one side as on the other. People took it for granted,
on principle, that this love was pure, platonic (and
sometimes it was). People, moreover, took it for
granted that this love was the only true love. Whence
that strange ruling of one of the Supreme Courts of
Love ("Courts" were, in truth, almost necessary to
support the laws and the rites of a love so strange and
so new) that love was incompatible with marriage;
since in marriage the husband continued to be the master of the woman—a situation not to be reconciled
with this new manner of envisaging love. An aristo-

cratic conception! A conception that could govern the manners and customs only of a narrowly aristocratic and exclusive society, but which gradually made its way into all classes!

So it came about that the feudal system contributed powerfully toward establishing between the sexes, at least so far as love was concerned, an equality which had not existed previously. It helped to create in men toward the women they loved (their "mistresses"), sentiments of tenderness, devotion and respect, which had not existed before. We may even make a further guess of great plausibility: this new conception of the veneration due to women as ladies and "mistresses," helped to consolidate, if not to establish, the cult of the Virgin Mary: virgin, but also "Our Lady"! Certain it is that not until this period do we find Her mentioned as *domina*.

It is apparent, lastly, that the feudal system gave us the novel as we still know it, the novel as we still insist that it shall be: a story in which there are men and women equally autonomous, equally free; a story in which there is adultery, too much adultery, but at any rate, love; a story of sentimental "situation" where conflicts of interest give rise to conflicts of passion. Along toward the close of the Middle Ages the aristocratic "romance of chivalry" (so-called because replete with adventures, sword-slashings, grand exploits, hair-raising journeys into lands that often did not exist —a truly illustrious ancestry for the humble adventure story of our day, so much decried in France) became a love story; and a love story it has in general remained.

The history of the novel in France becomes, therefore, the history of the evolution of sentiment—the sentiment of love. At the same time the history of the novel is the history of the evolution of society.

There is no help for it—the world is made that way. Sex is mixed inextricably with everything!

III

BEFORE AND AFTER LA PRINCESSE DE CLÈVES

NOTHING that has just been said about the influence of the "Courts of Love" and of the new conception of Love during the Middle Ages should be construed to mean that religious sentiment had no effects on the development of the novel in France. Mr. Ford Madox Ford, in "The English Novel," considers that this influence is shown in a notable and vigorous fashion in the early monuments of the English novel and of English literature—in Chaucer, Bunyan, Milton and many others. The statement is too obviously true to be disputed. But it is equally clear that religious concerns exerted their influence in two different ways. In the first place, society in those days, and English society in particular, was profoundly religious, and insisted on finding in literary works the reflection (in Shakespeare, but faintly discernible) of a daily and burning interest in things of the spirit. But, in the second place, there was not a little coercion. The Church, or perhaps we should say the Churches, said to writers of fiction, as Ford Madox Ford justly remarks: "We are too busy cutting one another's throats and inventing new theologies to bother with story tellers. You may write and compose what lay fiction you like; but the rack, the faggot, or the pillory, will attend you if you publish anything we don't like." Mr. Ford even suggests that Cervantes made his Don Quixote a poor lunatic in order to present certain bold and radical ideas under an apparently innocent garb. This is a plausible hypothesis—not more than that. All the same, I am greatly tempted to suppose that if *Gargantua* and *Pantagruel* had not been presented as a gigantic buffoonery, Rabelais might have experienced greater severity at the hands of the Church. As things turned out, he managed to die in time—the storm broke just afterwards!

I think it my duty to note here, parenthetically, that, in my opinion, *Gargantua* and *Pantagruel* are not novels, strictly speaking, any more than "Gulliver" is a novel. Like the work of the famous Irishman, they constitute a great, and a devastating, pamphlet. No love, no women—either in *Gargantua* or in "Gulliver"! Without women, without love, no novel!

It is certain, on the other hand, that the religious influence, the intention to "point a moral," is less apparent in the French novel than in the English. The heroes and heroines of our "romances of chivalry" are good Catholics. Men and women alike, they believe every last thing the Church teaches: they believe in the Sacraments, in the Resurrection, in Heaven, in Hell!

But all this believing has a very feeble influence on their thoughts and their conduct. They thrash Mohammedans. They make vows on saints' relics. They atone for crimes. They enter convents. But so far, nothing of importance!

The truth is that in those days there was no religious instruction for the laity at large. The Church was satisfied, so far as laymen were concerned, with the acceptance of the Church dogmas; and the laity, save for a few exceptions (heretics we have always with us), never even dreamed of disputing them. External mechanical submission was enough. It was only with the Reformation—and, of course, the Counter-Reform, the Catholic phase of the Reformation—that the laity began to take an interest in theological questions. It was only with the Reformation and the Counter-Reform that believing Christians—and at that time everyone believed—began taking daily and hourly pains to mix morals with religion, and to mold their conduct to their religious convictions.

But in literature proper there is mighty little of this. You will find no trace of moral and religious preoccupations in the *Astrée* of Honoré d'Urfé, a successor, in new manner, to the "romance of chivalry." There is no trace of them, either, in the novels of La Calprenède and of Mademoiselle de Scudéry. If there ever was such

a thing as a "society novel" these would be examples.
It is something almost incredible—yet the novels of
d'Urfé and La Calprenède were written, and passionately devoured, at the height of atrocious religious
wars; and those of Mademoiselle de Scudéry, when the
Fronde was in full swing, or at least when that period
of civil warfare was drawing to a close. A natural reaction perhaps? A desire in all minds to find in fiction
something to console them for realities, something to
bring "refreshment"? A little of each, most probably!
The tradition and the ideals of the "Courts of Love"
were still alive. An exclusive and aristocratic society,
brutal and vigorous, but living lavishly and on a noble
plane, felt a yearning for delicacy and refinement; an
ambition to distinguish itself by its manners and by its
ways of living, speaking, and loving, from the common herd.

This is, of course, a well-known fact, and many other
writers have noted it. And yet, perhaps it may not
be out of place to restate it here, just to remind ourselves that the "society novel"—if not the social novel
—is very old in France; that "romances of chivalry"
are themselves society novels as well as adventure
stories, and that the fiction of the early Seventeenth century is of the same character.

Meantime, the place which theological and religious

interests occupied in that society is perfectly apparent.
Even if the Abbé Brémond, in writings as distinguished
for their learning as for their feeling, had not acquainted us with the passion and depth of the religious
sentiment in France, the letters of Madame de Sévigné
alone, the books and the quarrels of Fénelon, Bossuet,
and Pascal, not to mention the great Jansenist free-for-
all, which lasted down to the French Revolution and
was not without a certain influence upon some phases
of the latter, would be sufficient proof. But if such in-
fluences be sought in our literature as literature, neither
in the novel nor in the drama (just the reverse of the
situation in England), do we find any striking traces
of them. As regards tragedy there is, to be sure, Corneille's *Polyeucte*, as well as other dramas with themes
borrowed from the "Book of Martyrs". There is Racine's *Esther*, there is his *Athalie*—both written to be
played for the exclusive benefit of demoiselles in board-
ing-school at Saint-Cyr—"amateur theatricals" so to
speak, not designed for the Broadway of those days.
Corneille, furthermore—and he is careful to apologize
—tried his hand at versifying a few lyrical passages
from the Old Testament. But in the novel, at least,
from any author whose name is still remembered, nothing, precisely nothing!

Yet we do find, at this time, a really distinguished

novel, the only one, or almost the only one, which has had readers all along down to our day, and the honor of frequent reprintings from generation to generation: *La Princesse de Clèves*. Here again we have a "society novel," but a more moral novel, a very moral novel indeed, pushing its eulogy of conjugal fidelity to the heroic, nay to the sublime! (A "society novel", therefore, beyond all question!)

The scene is laid at the Court of King Henry the Second. In certain features, and in spite of the fact that the majority of details are historically accurate, or virtually so, it strangely recalls the Court of Louis the Fourteenth. None but the most illustrious personages grace the stage. The milieu is the Court, nothing but the Court, a Court where men vie with one another in refinements of dress and niceties of language, in everything that can and ought to distinguish the courtier from the plain man. A moral novel, a very moral novel, it carries the same aristocratic distinction into the domain of morality.

Mademoiselle de Chartres (a great name and a great fortune) has married, without love, the Prince de Clèves. She falls desperately enamoured of the Duc de Nemours, who loves her to the point of madness. For her sake he renounces a plan to marry Elizabeth, Queen of England. Mademoiselle's mother endeavors to warn her daughter against such a guilty love. The mother dies. The Princess continues to resist her passion in spite of everything, even though M. de Clèves, whom she ends by marrying, believes her guilty (she gains nothing by her sacrifice). Deeply in love himself, irremediably humiliated at being the husband of a wife who does not requite him and has, as he thinks, betrayed him, M. de Clèves dies of grief. So now the Princess is free to yield to a passion which at last may be within the law. Far from her thoughts any such vulgar recourse: she will remain faithful, even beyond the grave, to the man whom she has never loved! She retires to a convent, which she will leave only for a short time each year to look after her property and devote herself "ever to concerns more holy than those of the severest cloisters."

I have quoted the last sentence in the novel. It is the only one that might justify us in attributing a religious motivation to the virtue of the Princesse de Clèves. Down to that last sentence there is not a word to reveal any such preoccupation. There is no question of "sin." The word "adultery" is not uttered once. We even fail to find a character one might have expected to appear at any moment—the father-confessor, the "spiritual director." In her death-bed admonishment to her daughter, the Princess's mother does not once mention the Commandments, hell-fire, or God. To be sure, the Princess must have been thinking of all these things: to be sure, a sturdy Christian upbringing must underlie her fidelity to her conjugal oath; *but it would have been vulgar to mention such a thing*!

To tell the truth, *La Princesse de Clèves* is still a sort of "romance of chivalry." Like a knight of the older days, the Princess aims at accomplishing "the most difficult thing of all," at winning a victory over herself, over her passion, just as a knight sought victory over some dragon or some Mohammedan infidel. In both cases the idea is to think and to act grandly! But what a difference in conception here as compared with "Tristan and Isolde," where passion is mistress, where the husband ends by resigning himself, by "understanding" the rights of passion—an echo of that morality of the "Courts of Love" which declared love incompatible with marriage.

In the Seventeenth century, on the contrary, Madame de Lafayette holds up before her sisters as the ideal of feminine heroism, as the ideal of all that is beautiful and great, a duty to struggle against passion and triumph over it, even carrying resistance to an extreme which common sense would term madness. . . . Just remember the very sensible—and very French—remark of a character in *Tristan*: "Dismeasure is not strength."

Here, in *La Princesse de Clèves*, there is visible "dismeasure." But dismeasure was the very thing that
stirred the reader of those days, especially the female
reader.

It follows, as we are constrained to note, that this
novel had no bearing on social realities. What the
morals of the time were may be seen in the "Little
Histories" of Tallement des Réaux (Protestant though
he was); in the "Archives of the Bastille," collected
by François Ravaisson (as regards everything concerning the "Poison Affair"); in the "Memoirs" left by a
curé of Versailles, who lived toward the end of the
reign of Louis the Fourteenth. The example of adultery
came from on high, from the king himself; and his
people acquiesced, with scarcely a murmur, when he
legitimatized his bastards. This same curé of Versailles
makes no effort to hide the "Corydonism" of a certain
stripe at Court, beginning with Monsieur, the King's
brother. On the vices of that gentleman we were already fully informed. What the venerable ecclesiastic
reveals is that he had many imitators. And, finally, the
police reports, in the "Archives of the Bastille," to
which I have referred, show that all too often the first
accusation which men of letters hurled at each other
in their private quarrels (not even the priests were
exempt) was the practice of "Socratism," a word that

could be spoken aloud long before "Corydonism" could be written in black and white. All of which, we may add, proves nothing, except that men in all ages and in all societies have possessed about the same amount of virtue and vice, the same amount of good and bad instincts.

But such things must not blind us to a fact that cannot be denied. In France as well as in the Protestant countries, the Seventeenth century was swept by an ardent and productive impulse toward religious revival. The Jesuits and the Jansenists, and more or less secret societies such as the *Confrérie du Saint-Sacrament*, all made themselves felt in different ways in that direction. The "Brotherhood of Christian Doctrine" offered elementary instruction, lay as well as religious and moral, to the poorer classes, while the Jesuits were trying to monopolize the education of the aristocracy and the bourgeoisie. The *Trappe de Rancé* revived and glorified asceticism. During this same period the *Congrégation de Saint-Sulpice* was established in order to develop a clergy learned in dogma and moral law; whereas, before that, the priests of the country districts and the small towns in the Provinces had been as ignorant and as little respected as the "popes" of modern Russia. The idea was a success! We need no further proof of that than the failure, under the Revolution, of the Civil Constitution of the Clergy, which tended to create a national church in France something like English Anglicanism. The constitution in question did not profess obedience to Rome. The petty clergy, therefore, refused to submit to it; and their parishes followed their lead—proof that in the course of a century, through the dignity of its manners and morals and the soundness of its supervision of souls, our clergy had acquired a prestige which it had never enjoyed previously! Our lower clergy, on the whole so unappreciated, counted for something in upholding religious sentiment in France all through the storm of the Revolution; and it also counted for something in the rise of literary Catholicism in the Nineteenth century. So, in literature, there are many facts, and important ones, which cannot be explained by a knowledge of literature only. To understand them requires knowledge of history—and history proper, the history of States and of societies. The late and much lamented Paul Souday made deliberate boast of ignoring history. That was one of the rare mistakes of that great exponent of "intellectualist" criticism.

I must ask the reader to forgive this lengthy digression. But was it not necessary to clarify certain aspects of my subject? What do we have in *La Princesse de Clèves*? A novel, a love-story, in which it would seem impossible to explain the heroine's victorious resistance to a requited passion, save as the result of absolute adherence on her part to the demands of Christian morality, and to inhibitions derived from that morality. And yet as I said, not a word suggesting Christianity! Not a word, down to the very last sentence, where the idea bursts forth: the woman had loved and had rejected a love that was within her reach. Yet she ended her life "which was somewhat brief" (what a delicate way of saying that she died of her renunciation!) "in concerns more holy than those of the severest cloisters, leaving behind inimitable examples of virtue!"

Here then we find a concern, an ambition, on the part of a woman to write a novel along the lines of the "romances of chivalry" and the "society novel," in which a woman would be made to accomplish in the feminine sphere a feat as difficult, as great, and as noble as warrior or knight ever achieved in the masculine sphere. But there is something else, probably: there is also the concept of the different literary *genres* as the latter were practised under the rules of French classicism down to and during the period of Romanticism, and (I believe) as they are still practised, under other forms, in our day. But in the Seventeenth century, the doctrine was pure, absolutely pure. Not only must tragedy not contain any comic elements, nor comedy any tragic elements: there are the "noble" *genres*, which are the *true* ones, and there are "vulgar" *genres*, which do not belong to literature. The "noble" *genres* are those which the ancients made illustrious: tragedy, for instance, and the epic. A work to be considered literary must have had a model and found a precedent in the classic eras of the two ancient literatures. It was because, perhaps only because, ancients like Theophrastus had written "characters," that La Bruyère's were regarded as "literature." History was a *true genre*, but history conceived in a certain manner, since "portraits" and harangues were essential. It was because such "portraits" existed in the ancient historians and in Plutarch that so many of them were written in the course of the Seventeenth and Eighteenth centuries, and probably for the same reason that our academic historians continue writing them today. But it should also be noted that life in society had made people aware of "psychology" and thus created a new art of history, just as the same "psychology" also created a new art in tragedy, making it something entirely different from the models supplied by the Greek masterpieces.

Now, for the novel, it chanced that that form of composition occupied only an inferior position in antiquity: it was a pastime—an ingenious pastime when practised by clever writers like Lucian or Apuleius, but a pastime for all that. A first consequence: none of the great writers of the Seventeenth century will write a novel (I sometimes think that Racine could have written a very fine one); and Voltaire, himself, in the century following, will write *Candide* and his other *Contes* only to amuse Madame du Châtelet and incidentally enlighten her on "optimism," or some other philosophical question. The novel, in Voltaire's eyes, was not "literature." Literature for him, was still tragedy, comedy, or history: not history as he wrote it in his *Essai sur les moeurs*, which seems, to us of his posterity, one of his greatest titles to glory; but history as he wrote it in his *Charles XII* and his *Age of Louis XIV*. The novel is left to second-rate scribblers, to a graphomaniac like the Abbé Prévost, who gives us *Manon Lescaut*, just badly written, among a host of downright stupidities: or to a fantastic dreamer such as Bernardin de Saint-Pierre, who can bring the taste of his time to accept the ingenuous and exotic spontaneities of *Paul and Virginia* only in view of that novel's humanitarian and philosophical content, which seemed at that moment the all-important thing.

Not only this—and here I come to my main point:

the theory of the *genres* prohibited the mingling of the sacred and the profane. Boileau interdicts such mixtures in vigorous language: the mysteries of religion do not seem to him proper subjects for literature; whether as a matter of reverence, or, what amounts to the same thing, because the artist can never feel sufficiently free in their regard. French society in the age of Louis the Fourteenth devoured the writings of theologians and religious pamphleteers. It had an enormous appetite for Arnault, Pascal, Fénelon, Madame Guyon and the "Apologetics" of Bossuet. It took as much interest in theology as we, in our time, take in politics and science, and probably more. It thought of its salvation just as assiduously, and with as much passion, as we think of the possibilities of improving humanity in material ways. But it would never have occurred to those people to mix literary amusements with "things of the faith"! The spheres were different!

There was, nevertheless, at that time one moralizing and social novel, of Utopian trend, which enjoyed an immense and enduring success; and it continues to hold its place among our school text-books: *Télémaque*. But *Télémaque* was written by a prelate for a child—a dauphin of France, therefore for educational purposes. And the prelate in question did not choose a Christian subject—Christian allusions are banned from *Télémaque*! Fénelon would never have dreamed of writing *Fabiola*! And notice another thing: all the way down to these latter days of ours, all the way down to M. Léon Bertrand and his *Sanguis martyrum*, the great Christian novels (with the single exception of Chateaubriand's *Martyrs*) have been English, Polish or Russian (Mérechkowsky with his *Julian the Apostate*), but never French!

From its very beginnings, English fiction has been imbued undisguisedly, avowedly, deliberately, with the spirit of Protestant Christianity, even when it has seen fit to combat hypocrisies in religion. Only through a similar attack on religious hypocrisy, in a *Tartuffe*, was a certain modicum of Christian spirit able to assert itself in our literature of the Seventeenth century; and *Tartuffe* is perhaps more soundly to be regarded as a protest from the "libertines". Still another reason for this difference between English literature and ours is that, in Catholic countries, the Church claims the monopoly of moral guidance of souls, whereas, in Protestant countries, that is the business of everybody.

But, on the other hand, in Catholic countries, at least in France, the practice of confession, and the resulting "examinations of conscience" may well have con-

tributed to some extent to developing a French psychological instinct, and an interest in the psychological
motivation of human action: whereas in Calvinist countries, or in sects closely related to Calvinism, the dogma
of justification may possibly have guided literature,
and more particularly fiction, toward subjective and
lyric moods. No intermediary between men (or
women) and God! If men (or women) remain believers and at the same time fall subject to great passions,
what tragic battles we may witness! If faith weakens,
then passion justifies itself, becomes God!

That is one of the favorite themes of French Romanticism. It came to us, through Byron among others,
from England. But while people in England were becoming more and more Protestant and moralistic, the
French *bourgeoisie* of the Nineteenth century, heir to
the French *bourgeoisie* of the Eighteenth century, took,
on the whole, very little stock in religion (and it is
the *bourgeoisie* that supplies the great majority of
French writers). The theme, therefore, produced more
numerous and more characteristic works in France than
in England. The novels of George Sand are the purest
type—I say "pure" in the etymological sense of the
word, "free from all alloy." Compare her novels with
the works of the Brontë sisters, for example. You will
see how, in the latter, the element of individual re

ligious control, unsupported by help or counsel from without, continues to assert itself energetically, and resists the doctrine of justification by passion alone.

Whether the Catholic confessional has exerted any influence on the psychological aspect of our literature, and of our fiction in particular, is a difficult question to answer. There may be such an influence, or, at least, there may have been. But Spain and Italy also have the Catholic confessional, and their novels are ordinarily much less psychological than ours. In the orthodox Catholicism of Russia the confessional does not play the important rôle it plays with us. Nevertheless the Russian novel is profoundly psychological, albeit in a very different fashion from the French.

One might also be tempted to suppose that if psychology holds so important a place in our literature, it is because the French are, in a special degree, a society people, finding particular enjoyment in social relations, in "conversation." To talk with people, we must know them; we become interested in knowing them better and better; we even demand that our writers have the art of explaining them to us. But was there ever a "society" in Russia? And yet Russia has a psychological fiction!

I am afraid, accordingly, that such conjectures are likely to turn out mere fancies, mere figments of thought. To insist on explaining everything is to end by explaining nothing! In such matters, it is the part of honesty to put forward "explanations" of which we are not absolutely sure only as hypotheses and suggestions!

IV

ENGLISH INFLUENCES ON THE FRENCH NOVEL

MR. FORD MADOX FORD is doubtless correct in warning us "that the Art of Writing is an affair as international as are all the other arts." "Flaubert," he asserts, "could never have written *Madame Bovary* had there not been before then *Clarissa Harlow* by Richardson. Nor yet could Conrad have written *Lord Jim* without Daudet's *Jack.*"

It strikes me that, in using just these words, Mr. Ford is making what the English call a "sweeping assertion." It is not at all certain that Flaubert was directly influenced by *Clarissa Harlow*. But Emma Bovary undoubtedly was, though probably the name of Richardson's heroine never reached her ears! Such was the atmosphere, still, as late as her day! Women were Clarissas and Pamelas, without knowing why! This is perhaps the nearest approach we can make to the truth. There are books like that, books of which we have never read a line, but which were internationally famous in their time, worked their way into the bone and blood of our mothers and grandmothers, and became the inspiration of conscious and unconscious imitators without end. Such books, quite beyond will of ours, leave traces in us, and all the stronger since they have never been "just literature" in our eyes.

Nor could one assert positively that Conrad's *Lord Jim* owes anything to Daudet's *Jack*, any more than one could positively assert (as was first quite plausibly supposed and then, in view of matters of date, disputed) that Daudet's *Jack* derives from Dickens's *David Copperfield*.

One thing is certain, however; the very considerable influence of the English novel on our literature and principally on our fiction. It is an influence of fairly remote date! There may be traces of Richardson in Diderot's *Neveu de Rameau*: Mr. Ford will have it that way, though, I confess, I do not discern it very clearly myself. But English influence is apparent enough in *Jacques le Fataliste*, and there the author was directly inspired by Stern's *Sentimental Journey*. And Rousseau! Rousseau himself! For thirty years past, Mr. Mornet has been noting the reminiscences, not to say the borrowings, which *Clarissa Harlow* contributes to Rousseau . . . *Clarissa Harlow* again! And Chateaubriand? From him, Mr. Ford quotes the following sentence, which is, for that matter, a beauty: "How sad it is to think that eyes too old to see, have not yet lost their capacity for tears!" Would it ever have been writ-

ten, asks Mr. Ford, had the great magician of style, the
sublime rhetorician who sleeps his last sleep, in pride
and solitude, on the rocks of Grand-Bé (and from
whom Barrès, in his turn, took many lessons) not been
stirred to the depths by Pamela?

Mr. Ford cites no further examples of English influence on our novel. He could have multiplied them
to infinity. That influence only increased with the dawn
of the Nineteenth century. Let my reader recall the
vast numbers of *émigrés* who crossed the Channel after
1790 and returned to France, some not till under the
First Empire, others not till after the reestablishment
of the old monarchy, in 1814. I do not say that they
discovered England. That would be going too far. For
one thing, we have just seen that the influence of Richardson on French writers and novelists of the Eighteenth century had been so profound that its indirect
consequences reached even to Flaubert. Then again, the
émigrés of the Revolution kept to themselves, taking
very little interest, for the most part, in British politics
and British life, only half understanding them, if they
achieved that much (like many Russians of our day
who have come to seek shelter in France since the
Soviet Revolution).

But something those *émigrés* did bring back to us:
in their heads, a knowledge "of the English language,

which twenty years of sojourn in England had compelled them to learn; and in their trunks, the novels of Walter Scott and the poems of Byron."

Unless we take account of Byron and the revelation his poems were for us; unless we take account of the pride, the despair and the spirit of moral rebellion with which his poems are imbued; and unless we take account of Ossian (I was about to forget that curious hoax of Macpherson, whom everyone admired and whom Napoleon himself ranked on a par with Homer, or even higher than Homer, and who brought it about that in our day still French babies are being baptized with the name of Oscar!), certain aspects of French Romanticism are utterly unintelligible. If Byron had not existed, or if the French had not read him, there would, no doubt, have been a French Romanticism all the same! But it would have been a different Romanticism. Is a proof required of the popularity of Byron's works in our country? *Manfred* was to be found in our five cent library—in the days when the five cent library still was!

But for Walter Scott it would be impossible to account for certain characteristics, if not essential, aspects which the French novel of the Restoration period, and of the period that followed, assumed. Here is a problem for us indeed! The novels of Walter Scott—even the best, even the *Antiquary*, *Quentin Durward* or *Rob Roy* seem to us today, if not altogether unreadable, at least naïve, or even childish. Not so for our grandfathers! In Balzac's *Lost Illusions*, Lucien de Rubempré arrives in Paris with the manuscript of the *Archer de Charles IX*, a mosaic of plagiarisms from *Quentin Durward*. But that is nothing! Had it not been for Walter Scott, would Mérimée ever have written the *Chronique de Charles IX*, or Hugo, *Notre-Dame de Paris*? In ten, in twenty places, Hugo proclaims his admiration for Walter Scott. Scott indeed is one of the few to whom he deigns to confess that he owes a little! And expressions of a similar admiration, a similar enthusiasm, recur, even more frequently perhaps, in the writings of Balzac.

Richardson in the Eighteenth century, Walter Scott in the Nineteenth, lie at the fountain-head of the French novel. And I think it possible to discern the reason why. It was England that first recognized the novel as a *genre*, a distinguished *genre*, a great *genre*. This was a revelation to French writers; for in a novel you could say what you had to say, and a lot besides, and much better than in a play. So it came about that the novel was established as a *genre*, and crystallized as a *genre* in very much the form in which we know it today. The extent of our debt to the Anglo-Saxons is quite apparent

—not forgetting, meantime, Goethe's *Werther*. Even Stendhal, whose work shows no trace of reminiscence or imitation, whether of Richardson or of Walter Scott, goes to the trouble, in several places in his correspondence, of recording the deep impression which those predecessors of his across the Channel had made on him.

But there was something else that helped to lift the French novel to the dignity of a great *genre*: the *Nouvelle Héloïse*.

V

LA NOUVELLE HÉLOÏSE

IT BEING my bounden duty to point out the debt which the French novel owes to England, a fact too generally overlooked, I was almost obliged to exaggerate a little. Of course in a literature as rich, as ancient, as substantial, as original as ours, foreign influence can at the most act only as a catalytic, coordinating, perhaps transfiguring in aspect, elements already existing. That one of the "sources" of inspiration in Rousseau's *La Nouvelle Héloïse* may be found in *Clarissa Harlow* is a fact superabundantly demonstrated. None of the so-called "critical" historians of our literature has the slightest doubt on the issue. But there was Rousseau himself! We would not be reckless, nor even extreme, in asserting that the French novel, such as it has remained, the novel which is no longer "society," but social, the "novel of reform," and further (and above all) the "novel of passion," date from the *Nouvelle Héloïse.*

"A great book," said M. Victor Giraud, "a date of importance in the history of French fiction, and even in the history of the French mind." Such a statement must prove, at first blush, disconcerting—I speak for myself, at least. Certainly down to our day, the *Nou-*

velle Héloïse has had passionate admirers. There is the famous remark by Eugène Melchior de Voguë, a man by no means lacking either in intelligence or in sense of art, since it was he who opened the eyes of France to the Russian novel: "The years when I reopen *La Nouvelle Héloïse*, I cannot long endure any other novel."

I confess that I have difficulty in agreeing with him. Julie, the divine Julie, with her "bitter kisses"; the enterprising lover Wolmar; the insufferable and falsely virtuous Saint-Preux (for that matter they are all falsely virtuous—a thing that caps the climax of the reader's irritation), talk interminable bosh and exchange letters that obviously were never written. No human being could possibly have written them; no human being would have read them! Frankly, the novel, the illustrious novel, bores me beyond endurance! "Verbose and brainless maniacs!" decides M. Victor Giraud; and I can only agree with him in such a drastic judgment.

But there is worse! Dissertations on gardening, on botany, on the education of children, on political economy and the government of States! Six volumes of such, in the original edition! It is staggering! Though I cannot agree with M. de Voguë, I heartily approve of Taine: "*La Nouvelle Héloïse* is a bad novel; but its worst defect is the melody of its periodic sentences. . . . Far-fetched contrasts, plain words studiedly

avoided, an everlasting rhythm to express the abandon-
ment and the violence of soulful emotions . . . a
learned style is not compatible with noble thoughts!"

And yet, and yet, in spite of that—seventy editions
in forty years—an enormous figure for that time! A
wild success everywhere! Not only the aristocracy and
the rich *bourgeoisie*, but the plain folks—mechanics,
watchmakers, cabinet-makers—begin writing "verbosi-
ties" like Saint-Preux, and their wives and daughters,
like Julie. . . . And later on, the men of the Revolution will utter long rolling sentences in the style of
Rousseau even in the solemn and tragic hours of their
death. The *Nouvelle Héloïse* is in their blood! They
exude it through every pore! What can all that mean
if not that Rousseau had not only discovered, or re-
discovered, a "sensibility" which the intellectualism of
the Eighteenth century had smothered, but had revealed a new conception of love, the irresistible divine,
imperious rights of love, as opposed to all social constraints and triumphing over such constraints?

That the pretentious, unnatural periods and "ca-
dences" in the style of the *Nouvelle Héloïse* make bitter copy for the modern reader, that they even seem
ridiculous to us, I shall not be the one to deny. But
just how far are they responsible for the admirable,
the sublime, sentences of Chateaubriand, and, through

Chateaubriand, for the more condensed, the more vigorous sentences of Flaubert?

In this connection, I must venture a remark! Down to the end of the Middle Ages, the language our writers used was purely analytical. It progressed in short, sometimes incoherent and confused sentences, according as the author was more or less awkward. But with the Renaissance, and the recovery and assiduous study of Greek and Latin authors, Latin especially, our language begins aspiring to the synthetic character of the ancient tongues, and more particularly to the oratorical style—the cadenced period. Even Voltaire in his time will make concessions to such demands when he feels that the *genre* is "noble." But in general, under pressure of intellectualism, philosophical rationalism, and of a deeper instinct for the true genius of our language as well, the Eighteenth century ordinarily reverts to the analytical style.

Rousseau breaks this current. His style becomes oratorical again; and so the style of the great Romanticists, of Victor Hugo himself, will be. Flaubert likewise; though, after all, in his time, the two currents will be running side by side. Stendhal in his "writing" remains Eighteenth century—analytical, that is; though in thought, in subject matter, and in manner of conceiving the latter, he becomes passionately Romanticist.

Saint-Preux, in the novel, is Rousseau, the ingenuous and low-lived Rousseau, who says to Mme. d'Houdetot (Julie is a synthesis of all the women Rousseau loved and most often failed to possess: Mlle. Galley, Mlle. de Graffenried, Mme. Bazile, Mme. de Larnage, Mme. de Warens, but above all Sophie d'Houdetot): "I do not ask you to give up your lover Saint-Lambert" (Wolmar, in the novel)! "Far from me a thought so dishonoring, so contrary to virtue! But love me too, in some other way: platonic, perhaps—but not quite platonic: æthereally, sensuously!" All of which we may call flat, banal, not to say depressing. And yet, a strange thing! When the novel first appeared no one found it that way (even we moderns have to make an effort to do so). People found *La Nouvelle Héloïse* a drama of passion, where all the protagonists are heroes of virtue, as in *La Princesse de Clèves* (much less elegantly, of course); so true is it that our literature was long beset by the obsession of the heroic, the superhuman, the difficult. But they also found in it a physiological, carnal element, a proclamation of "the right to love," which is the flat opposite of the moral tension in the *Princesse de Clèves*, and was destined to leave deep marks on the novelists who were to follow.

Despite all that, the contemporaries of Jean-Jacques were not mistaken as to the general bearing of the book. In itself it was a revolution. As M. Victor Giraud very correctly asserts: "It established the novel as a dignified work of art, made it a vehicle for thought, capable of dealing with all questions of interest to mankind, and of stating and debating problems of conscience. . . ."

Rousseau, we may say, created the formula of the modern novel. Almost all the features which fiction has been presenting for some two centuries past—the "character novel," the "lyrical novel," the "analytical novel," the "society novel," the "novel of ideas," the "thesis-novel," the "religious novel," and the "novel of reform"—all have their common origin in *La Nouvelle Héloïse*.

Had it not been for the horticultural, the sociological, the economic, ramblings in the *Nouvelle Héloïse*, would Balzac ever have dared to venture his own long, too long, dissertations on politics and religion? Would Hugo ever have dared to insert his essay on printing (*Ceci tuera cela*) in *Notre-Dame-de-Paris*; or, in *Les Misèrables*, his endless chapter on the sewers of Paris, which made Hugo one of the men most responsible for the modern system of sewage disposal in the French capital? I could mention many other examples.

And how many themes of *La Nouvelle Héloïse* have been used over and over again by Rousseau's successors! The theme of the "poor young man" among others! It is as a hired tutor that Saint-Preux gains access to his Julie and falls in love with her. Mr. Victor Giraud endeavors to enumerate the number of times this situation has since been exploited: Octave Feuillet's *The Romance of a Poor Young Man* precisely; Cherbuliez's *Count Kostia*; Pierre Benoit's *Koenigsmark*; and even *The Disciple* by Paul Bourget! And yet Mr. Giraud forgets the most glorious and the most beautiful of these quasi-reminiscences: Julien Sorel in Stendhal's *The Red and the Black*, who gains access to Mme. de Rênal also as a tutor! If, as appearances indicate, we owe Julien's "introduction" to the involuntary suggestion of some long-forgotten reading of *La Nouvelle Héloïse*, that debt alone would exact of us an eternal gratitude to Jean-Jacques Rousseau! As for Bourget, he must have been thinking of Julien Sorel rather than of Saint-Preux, in sketching the tutor in *The Disciple*. He was too devoted to *The Red and the Black*—he had read it too often, not to have had it in mind!

So it goes in literature! Types change in aspect from generation to generation; but they retain the fundamental traits which their first great creators stamped on them!

VI

AFTER ROUSSEAU

ROUSSEAU may therefore be considered the inventor of the novel in France. Since his time, the *genre* has developed tremendously. I have not consulted statistics, but it would seem, from a survey of the windows in the bookshops, that the production of fiction, at all times abundant, has increased some tenfold in our country since the war.

In this respect our age may be compared with the one that followed the fall of the First Empire, from 1815 to 1830. In lesser proportions there was at that time a florescence of fiction very much like the one we observe today. I have mentioned that Balzac, in *Lost Illusions*, shows us handsome Lucien de Rubempré's début in life facilitated by the success of the *Archer of Charles IX*, a novel which that young man had brought to town from the country in his valise. Balzac was hardly exaggerating—great creators rarely exaggerate: they merely draw individual or social traits in stressed lineaments that remain unforgettable. And it is certain that, under Louis the Eighteenth and Charles the Tenth, there appeared, in far greater numbers than at any other moment in our history, writers who had a real talent, and others who had less, but who none the less got themselves printed and read. Of the era of the Restoration we chiefly remember, it is true, our poets and our dramatists. At that time the renaissance in literature extended to all the *genres*, and Romantic drama and Romantic poetry burgeoned forth with merits frequently lacking in many Restoration novels. These were indeed Romantic, but they had, as a rule, a certain "troubadourish" tone, or else were dyed in too black a gloom. Hugo's *Hans of Iceland* is an example. Hans drinks "the blood of men and the brine of the seas" from a human skull—and, despite the admiration I profess for the giant of Romanticism, what can I do but titter?

For this florescence of fiction, under the Restoration, there were several causes. I make no pretense of distinguishing them all. Here nevertheless are a few that strike the most casual glance.

Whatever the Liberals of those days may say, the censorship was much more lenient under the Restoration than under the First Empire. This was certainly true of the novel and the stage; and I believe it was of newspapers. Newspapermen and song-writers were censored and thrown into prison. Newspapers were fined, suspended, or even suppressed. But there were still newspapermen, and there were still newspapers:

under Napoleon the First there were none at all! But the freedom left to books was broader than the more or less restricted freedom left to periodicals; and this semi-compression was bound to find compensation in a sort of explosion.

As I have just suggested, we must also take into account the return of the *émigrés*, and the better knowledge of contemporary English literature and the influence of Walter Scott and Byron, resulting. But in addition, the Revolution had given rise to a new society, while an older one still existed. Nothing ever dies so very quickly! The old society had merely been shorn of the political power it had exercised through "the Court"—that is, through those who could approach the King and exert influence upon him. That exclusive power had now passed into the hands of a rich *bourgeoisie*—landowners especially, bankers and manufacturers more rarely. It held its sway through the agency of a Parliament over which, by virtue of the prevailing suffrage laws, the same wealthy *bourgeoisie* had exclusive control. Nevertheless, the old aristocratic society still survived, in its men and in its manners, particularly in the provinces. And there was still a fairly large number of titled landowners, either of the ancient nobility or of the nobility Napoleon had endeavored to create, who held seats in the two houses of Parliament.

The result? Two concomitant, though inverse, developments! Those ghosts of the Past, returning to earth in a new world, surviving like foreign bodies encysted in a growing organism, needed to know their new environment. And on the other hand, the younger generation which was beginning to write, young people who had grown up after the revolutionary whirlwind, but had witnessed, under the Empire, the death agonies of the old society, were now expressing, or trying to express, their new aspirations, their new conceptions of men, women, institutions, love. They attacked or admired the old society. But whether they attacked or admired it, they found it fascinating, advertised it, held it up as a rare, precious, and still living institution which seemed triumphant again throughout the rest of Europe (the Europe of Metternich), and, supported by "throne and altar," might come to life again in France despite the efforts of "Liberalism."

Born under Jean-Jacques, Romanticism had attained a magnificent adolescence, and proclaimed itself a literary revolution, under Chateaubriand. In these circumstances it now came into vigorous, though not very clear, self-consciousness. As always happens when one is too close to things, when one is "in" things, this new Romanticism was not very sure just where it was headed. It felt things more clearly than it comprehended them.

There was a counter-revival, in progress since the days of Chateaubriand (and others—the anti-romantic Laharpe, for example), of a certain literary Catholicism or literary Christianity strangely colored and adulterated, to be found foreshadowed already in Rousseau. There was an enthusiastic, youthful admiration for the glories of the Revolution and of the First Empire, which people were inclined to confuse one with the other (during the first fifty years of the Nineteenth century people discerned, more clearly than we do today, that Napoleon was the successor and the "adaptor" of the Revolution). A certain pride was rampant in all classes at finding public offices now open to everyone. Writers and artists, at the same time, were nursing feelings of disdain for the *"bourgeois,"* whom the Revolution was making a dominant class, and who were extending their conquests: it was the literature of the early Nineteenth century that devised the literary theme of scorn for the *"bourgeois,"* the *"bourgeois"* as a class. In the old days it had made game only of upstarts, like Turcaret —the *nouveaux-riches* of our time. Intellectuals and artists were vaguely perceiving that they were a sort of wedge thrust in between the climbing *bourgeoisie* and an aristocracy that was struggling to hold its place. That was why the practise of duelling sprang up among artists—duelling had formerly been the exclusive privilege of aristocracy. They were proud of the noble birth they eyed with envy, and often usurped it: the son of Musset-Pathay became Alfred de Musset; Balzac, a descendant of humble peasants in Auvergne, became Honoré *de* Balzac, and he assumed the arms and the crest of the *de* Balzacs d'Entragues! And yet, if not a few leaned toward literary or even political Christianity, others remained imbued with the philosophical doctrines of the Eighteenth century. Continuing as aristocratic and snobbish in their tastes as their colleagues in reaction, they were, like the *bourgeois* of the day whom they abominated, "anti-clericals." The domination of the clergy and the Jesuits, on whom the Restoration, especially under Charles the Tenth, tried to find support, was an object of loathing to them. Like the protagonists of the Revolution, they showed mercy only on the Jansenists, who were again being persecuted.

Two great novelists were soon to begin publishing: Balzac and Stendhal. Each was to manifest one of these tendencies: Balzac will be a monarchist and a Catholic; Stendhal will be a liberal and an anti-clerical.

After the lapse of a century, such things seem hardly important in our eyes. We are interested only in their genius, which was incomparable. Yet the point has to be borne in mind.

VII

BALZAC

SIXTEEN years old at the time of Waterloo! Thirty-one in 1830! The year before he had already published *The Last Royalist* (*Le Dernier Chouan*) and, from that date to 1847, the ninety-seven volumes of the *Comédie Humaine*! The last two volumes, appearing in 1847, almost contemporaneously with the fourth part of *Splendors and Miseries of Courtesans*, are *Cousine Bette* and *Cousin Pons*: two masterpieces after so many others—after *Père Goriot, Colonel Chabert, The Lily of the Valley, The Antiquary's Shop, A Shady Affair, César Birotteau, Eugénie Grandet*! And there were found among his papers the titles of fifty-one others, which death alone—not any enfeebling of imagination or genius—prevented him from writing!

"A huge person, florid, high-colored; black hair, tossed back like a horse's mane; small but very keen eyes—the eyes of an elephant or a wild boar; three chins, and, without exaggeration, the appearance of a stout pork-packer!" . . . Such the portrait Gozlan draws of Balzac, and all contemporaries agree with Gozlan. A common person, very common; short in stature, "small" in his ways, noisy, chattering, clowning, swaggering; and a snob to boot—as much of a snob as Marcel Proust will be, later on! The Duchess de Castries—who will be the Duchess de Langeais in his novels—is to Balzac what the Duchess de Guermantes will be to Proust; but Balzac is earnestly, seriously, madly, in love with her; for he is a male, a male of tremendous appetites, and all sorts of appetites—the Duchess d'Abrantès, the Princess Bagration, the Countess Merlin, and finally the Countess Hanska, will be well informed on that point. And consider the dedications of his novels and his short stories! Almost all are addressed to the great of the earth! Greedy for distinctions, titles of nobility, the Academy, and for money —easy money!

Balzac was what may be called a mythomaniac. He was incapable of distinguishing between reality and the world—the truly vast world—inhabited by the two thousand characters who crowd the *Comédie Humaine*. He thinks he has given a white horse to Jules Sandeau! The pineapples of Ville-d'Avray will net him 100,000 francs! He meets Henri Monnier on the steps of the Bourse and says: "I have a scheme that is going to earn me just fourteen millions!" And Monnier, holding out his hand: "Fine, advance me a hundred *sous* on the profits!" We have all heard such stories of Balzac. But his best remark of the kind is perhaps one he never uttered, one that was merely attributed to him. On his deathbed he says: "Call Bianchon! He is the only one who can save me!"

Horace Bianchon was a doctor in the *Comédie Humaine*. He never existed, save in Balzac's imagination, and was partly borrowed from Broussais at that! Notice, however, that Balzac created the type in our literature and it has since become a commonplace: the physician, profound and unselfish, the apostle of secular salvation.

But what a strange mythomaniac! No one was ever more dependent upon the reality which he transfigures —on what he considers reality, at least! No one before him, and perhaps after him, took more trouble to equip himself with information, with "documents." It is probable that the Goncourts, who are supposed to have founded our "documentary school," were inspired by Balzac. All the journeys he took, all his "notes from nature," all his landscapes! As early as the *Last Royalist*, one of his first novels, he may be found researching at Fougères. . . . Some twenty-five years ago I retraced Balzac's footsteps in that neighborhood one by one. And how exact, how clear, his vision! It was enough to drive one mad—any writer will understand what I mean! I could find nothing more to say, nothing to add; not only as regards the things, the aspects of nature, that were to be seen, but as regards the seeing itself! Just reread Lenôtre, or Emile Gabory (that remarkable local historian, too little known, who wrote *La Guerre des Géants*) in his *La Vendée et la Révolution*! They only confirm Balzac. We may suspect that Lenôtre, a man of culture and literary imagination, may have been influenced by Balzac. But this evidently is not the case with Gabory. And yet Balzac made a novel of all that, a Romantic novel, *à la* Walter Scott! Observations, memories, "they-says," form the thread of the story. But what a difference, in Balzac's favor, between his talent and that of the Scotchman!

Sometimes, as in *La Messe de l'Athée*, these memories, this gossip, may be traced: we know whence they came. And again at other times, as in the admirable *Colonel Chabert*, we do not know. But we may be certain that they existed. And they are all transformed, magnified, recreated, gigantic, living!

Now as M. Pierre Abraham lucidly and accurately remarks (in a very concise *Balzac*, replete nevertheless with erudition and suggestions), not only these memories, these "they-says," in large part, but the very conception that Balzac has of society, of his duties, of his norms, come from the Restoration, from the period that stretches between 1815 and 1830. And from this period date his Catholic and monarchical convictions. M. Pierre Abraham calls all that "servility"—not, for that matter, in any ill-humor; just as he calls the mythomania, quite frankly, an instinct for lying. I have no objection to the use of plain everyday language in place of self-styled scientific terms. There is, however, a difference. In Balzac, the lie was disinterested, and his "servility" likewise.

This, quite simply, is what happened. Between sixteen and thirty, the years when people feel, as well as observe, Balzac had lived under the Restoration and accepted the principle on which the Restoration was based, as a fact and as a social and political ideal (he is no more to be reproached for that, from the literary point of view, than is Zola for having accepted republican and democratic ideas). He not only described the society of the Restoration, therefore; he also considered it the best of societies—taking things as they were at a time when, not writing as yet, at the most hastily composing novels that did not "turn out," he had the time to observe.

This may perhaps explain why Balzac's society, at the time "imaginary" (we have just seen to what extent: "imaginary," because the author was a man of imagination!), scarcely put in an appearance, in actual history, as M. Paul Bourget remarks, until after the novelist's death. The true Balzacian society would be that of the Second Empire! The true de Marsay would be the Duc de Morny, the true Marcas, Gambetta! That the influence of Balzac's work was considerable, that people made an effort to model themselves on it, is indisputable. Pierre Louys has succeeded in deciphering some manuscript memoirs, skilfully written in cryptograph, and relating precisely to the period of the Second Empire. All the people in them endeavor to play rôles from the *Comédie Humaine!* But another reason may have been that Balzac had divined what the society of the Restoration was going to produce. He saw into the future!

Let us accordingly consider that society with him, along with what we know of it now from other sources. What had changed in France between the Revolution and the year 1830 was the political and administrative structure of the country, not its economic structure, and, consequently, not the terms of individual existence. The people Balzac knew lived in the same ways, exactly, as people had lived in the Eighteenth century. None of the great scientific discoveries made by his time had as yet been practically applied. The French were still a people of peasants, small artisans in little factories, shopkeepers. People travelled in the same diligences. They used the same "Chappe Telegraph." They had the same ways of earning money and spending it. Money came partly from commerce, partly from investments, and, to a large extent, from land. "Big business," which was being made possible by coal and steam, was still in its infancy. It was hardly adolescent even under the Second Empire. Not before the year 1889, as René Boylesve points out, did French society begin to change as a consequence of the increasing numbers of great fortunes resulting from "big business" and large-scale finance.

Herein lies the powerful appeal of Balzac's work and the reason why people have been able to read it for so long a time. It was still something up to date. The railroad was the only practical invention important enough to change manners and customs by facilitating communications between province and province, nation and nation, and favoring growth in the populations of large towns. There were still country districts which railroads did not reach, and which remained as they had been before, or very nearly so. Add to this that there came a reinforcement of conservative tendencies as a result of the concerted action, in the educational field, of Congregations which were more or less favored, before being more or less persecuted, under the Second Empire and at the beginning of the Third Republic. Religious education helped to maintain old customs and ideas, and old conceptions of sex morality, especially among women, who were educated al-

most altogether in convents. That is why, even as late
as thirty years ago, the *Lily of the Valley* could still
be considered by the French a breviary of their aspirations, their remorses, and their manner of envisaging
love.

The French world, such as Balzac saw it, lasted, in
other words, a very long time. And it still endures, in
spite of telephones, autos, moving pictures, Communism, and all that economic overturn which was in
preparation before the World War and which the consequences of the War have merely precipitated. The
French remain, in the majority, a people of small rural
landowners and, as in Balzac's day, they continue struggling with what is left of large landed property and
with the clergy, which, down to very recent times,
continued resting its weight on the aristocracy of land
and made common cause with it. So it is that, in the
small towns of our provinces and in our country districts, the ways in which human passions manifest
themselves have not greatly changed in a century past.
Because a peasant uses a tractor instead of an ox it
does not follow that he has changed in his deeper
essence; he remains what he was, conservative (that is
to say, a partisan of the established order, as against
the Socialists, and of "property"; but a partisan of *his*
property; in other words, of "small," not of "big"

property). He is a Malthusian. He is an anti-clerical. He is fundamentally individualistic, moreover. And, though he limits the number of his children, he cherishes firm and definite convictions as to the ancient traditions of the family, of the child's duty of obedience to the parent, and the wife's duty of submission to her husband. Keep these traits in mind and then tell me whether, even after the Great War, which seems to have been less destructive to the old, absolutist Germany than to what was left of great rural property in France, a novel such as *Les Paysans* does not still seem to have been written yesterday!

But what, after all, is the importance of this social interest, or if you prefer—using a horrible word that compromises and even dishonors an artist—this sociological interest in Balzac? What does it matter that the "high society" described by Balzac is (if we take it seriously) the society of a Restoration which, essaying to resuscitate a dead thing, and to make of that dead thing an imitation of aristocratic society in England, succeeded in producing only a caricature of the latter with traits which will be still further exaggerated in the truly Balzacian epoch, that of the Second Empire? The essential thing is something quite different: the creation, namely, the life that is portrayed, a vast, teeming life, a super-reality! The philosopher Ravaisson has said that the true work of art is not a form, but the deep underlying cause whence all forms proceed. The sublime paradox of a Platonist—true with a transcending truth! So it is with the types of Balzac: Baron Hulot, Cousin Pons, *le père* Goriot, *le père* Grandet, Mme. Marneffe, Mme. de Mortsauf (the two antipodes, these, of feminine nature). These people are universal types, on the same grounds and in as absolute a fashion, as Molière's Harpagon or Racine's Phèdre. And if they exist in the same inevitable manner it is for the same reason. The variety of incidents to which they give rise, or which they encounter, permit the development of the most comprehensive "commonplaces" conceivable—I am using the term "commonplace" in its original, honorable, even highly flattering sense, which ordinary usage has lamentably diverted from the earlier acceptation. In literature we must understand it to mean characters, passions, and the shock of events resulting from those particular characters and passions, which pack a work with the strongest total of emotion and interest which the greatest possible number of readers can experience. Balzac's writing endures immortal by virtue of its great "common-places," its multiplicity of "universal" characters. Grandet is avarice, or rather the passion for money and power through money. Goriot is fatherly affection. Esther is

the enamoured courtesan (the great "commonplace"
invented by Romanticism). Baron Hulot is senile lust.
Mme. de Mortsauf (in the *Lily of the Valley*) imper-
sonates the victorious and fatal struggle of virtue—or
rather duty—against love and desire. Notice just here
that the subject of the *Lily of the Valley* is exactly the
same as that of the *Princesse de Clèves*. But there are
two differences: in the first place, the injunctions of
Catholic morality openly play a rôle in Mme. de Mortsauf's decision not to give herself to the man she loves;
whereas, in the *Princesse de Clèves*, these injunctions
are hidden from view. In the second place, Mme. de
Mortsauf dies quite as much out of jealousy of her
rival, Lady Dudley, as out of love pure and simple.
And another thing: in *La Princesse de Clèves*, all the
characters—the wife, the husband, the unhappy lover
—are heroes, more heroic than people ordinarily are.
In the *Lily of the Valley* the only full-fledged heroine
is the wife. The unhappy lover is only a semi-hero:
very humanly he takes a mistress less platonic than his
adored Henriette. As for the husband, he is shown to
us—one of the tricks of Romanticism—as frankly insufferable and not deserving of the harsh sacrifice that
is made for him.

But Goriot, Grandet, Pons, Mme. Marneffe, poor
Henriette, even Rastignac and Vautrin, the escaped

convict: all are heroes, now in crime, now in virtue, now in ambition. That is to say, they are greater than nature, carrying their vices, their virtues, their passions, farther than men ordinarily do—exactly like the people in the "romances of chivalry," in *La Princesse de Clèves*, in *La Nouvelle Héloïse*. You will not find this same trait in the characters of the English novel of the period, nor in the Russians of a later period. In Balzac's time it is still a purely French trait in the novel. Not without reason did the words "hero" and "heroine" come to be applied to the protagonists of fiction. The tendency toward heroism, toward something "greater than nature," will reappear in Hugo's *Les Misérables* (Jean Valjean and the detective Javert), and in the characters in *Ninety-three*. Romanticism exaggerated it, featured it more violently. But it had existed from the dawn of our literature, and may be easily detected in the second of our great novelists of 1830—Stendhal.

VIII

" AN ADVENTURER . . . who made a sort of reputation for himself by dint of intrigue and effrontery. . . . This individual who had just called quits with life was named Beyle, the only thing he had in common with the great scientist. Tossed out on the sidewalks of Paris, with a very debatable wit and without a shilling in his pocket . . . he became a caterer of literary anecdotes to a popular periodical; and when that market failed, he invented yarns for dinner tables. He sought an *alias* and chose the name of Stendhal, the German cast of which attests the nature of the literary sect which had adopted him. He finished by writing books. The one he called *La Chartreuse de Parme* made a certain reputation for him in the fairly populous world of mediocrities in contemporary literature. He did me the honor to speak of me once, and to write that I had not sufficient intelligence to understand the literary revolution that was going on about my little person. I had enough, however, to predict that it would not go far. Stendhal will have no more of a future than the second Beyle would have had, regardless of the applause from the Romantic slums which harbor the most credulous and brainless of all

75

literary and dramatic cliques. I forget how the subject came up one day when I was talking with M. Guizot, who had had some fairly warm relations with that coterie, and consequently must have known this scullion. 'He is a blackguard!' M. Guizot replied, and I did not go any further. An attack of apoplexy rid us of him on the twenty-fourth of March (1841)."

The incredible paragraph, which I have just quoted in full from the July number (1929) of the *Revue des Deux Mondes*, may be found in the *Mémoires* of M. Viennet, a member of the Académie Française, a former lieutenant-colonel of artillery, a courageous soldier (as his service papers testify), an excellent academician, I suppose, author of a tragedy *Arbogaste*, which no one ever heard of, and of *Promenades au Père Lachaise*, likewise forgotten, in spite of the macabre allurements of a title so surprising from the pen of such a furious adversary of Romanticism. No ferocity could be greater, nor, I might add, more unlucky—though perhaps I am mistaken in that. This passage in Viennet's *Mémoires* undoubtedly gives that poor man the only chance he could have had of surviving to posterity.

Nevertheless I should like to have been alive in those days—1842, when literary hatreds were strong enough to move a thoroughly excellent man to such harshness. Perhaps they were worth more, after all, than the general flabbiness, the universal soft-soaping, that is prevalent in our day. And yet the attack in itself is disgraceful. Hatred could be carried no further in words. But we must remember that, in France at least, literary animosities are even stronger than political hatreds. And the unfortunate Viennet was grossly mistaken: the Stendhal "who had no more future than the second Beyle" has been growing greater every day and is still growing: whereas Viennet. . . .

The author of *The Red and the Black* and of *La Chartreuse de Parme* was not a guttersnipe. He had been one of Napoleon's officers and was proud of his uniform as a Hussar. He shaved stoically every morning during the terrible campaign in Russia, and the Emperor, seeing him at it, said one day: "You are a brave man!" He got to be member of the Council of State, and proved an efficient functionary as tax collector at Sagan. Under Daru, moreover, he made an excellent foreign consul; though it was said of him (unfortunately, one of his successors at Trieste, M. Dollet, has destroyed the legend) that "there was nothing of the literary Bohemian, nothing even of the Bohemian, about him"—nothing, in short, calculated to distinguish him from the rank and file of the *bourgeoisie*. He was indeed—the trait is characteristic of his mind—very much the *bourgeois* of his day: he de-

spised the mob and envied the "great," with an ambition to join the latter; he was as anti-clerical, or rather
as anti-Jesuitical, as a plain Béranger; and he dreaded
(perhaps with good cause) the espionage of the police,
as did the majority of our grandfathers down to the
end of the Second Empire.

Nervous, but controlling himself, or trying to; feminine; timid as a woman; thinking only of voluptuousness, but timidly voluptuous (in such cases everything
turns to imagination!), Stendhal had the true temperament of the man of letters, of the literary creator. He
was a mad dreamer, as Balzac was (but in a different
way) and as are all great creators in literature. He
made far fewer conquests than he dreamed of making
—just the reverse, in this domain, of Balzac, who at
least was blessed with an immoderate appetite. But
such things, save for the chance insight they give, are
of minor importance. More important is his talent, his
genius, the part of him that is original and immortal
and will make all novelists—the best at least—his
debtors to the end of time.

He is supposed (though not till our day) to have
said of himself: "I shall not be read until about 1880."
He was not far wrong. It was Taine and Bourget who
put him in his proper place. And so the question arises
—a question that recurs periodically in all literary chat:

"In the huge pile of books that past generations have bequeathed to us, may there not be a few unknown masterpieces?" . . . I am inclined to believe, without very much proof, that there can be no good works that are entirely unknown. The good book is always recognized, at the moment of its appearance, by a few people of taste. The public may not "follow" at once; but the people of taste have passed on the countersign to subsequent generations, and these understand at last. However, there are books of an intermediary category, books that are too exceptional, too rare. The *Adolphe* of Benjamin Constant will always exert an immense and well-deserved influence on the psychology of the novel, without ever reaching a very wide audience. So also for the *Obermann* of Denancour, so valuable as a keen—and moreover psychological—manifestation of Romantic sensitiveness, of the supreme, extreme, and nevertheless inevitable consequences of Rousseau's influence! *Obermann* will never have the number of readers Stendhal, or even *Adolphe*, has had. It will merely continue arousing now the curiosity, now the interest, of a few people, and giving rise to university dissertations! It will never be entirely unknown, never entirely forgotten.

The very proper and very general admiration that is professed for Stendhal nowadays has tempted people to defend him even from the accusation of "writing badly." I consider Stendhal one of the greatest masters of fiction, one of the pinnacles of that kind of literature: but we must not let ourselves be blinded to what he actually is.

Stendhal declared that his idea was to write like the drafters of our Civil Code—not such a bad model after all! And it is apparent from all his work that in his choice of subjects, in the descriptions and the actions of his characters, in his very conception of a novel, Stendhal is Romantic, ultra-Romantic. On this point the splenetic Viennet was not mistaken. But, in his style, Stendhal, like Victor Jacquemont, like Mérimée (both friends of his), is the direct heir of the Eighteenth century; just as, in his opinions and what may be called, roughly, his anti-clericalism, he is the heir of Voltaire (much more than of Rousseau). But he is not, literally speaking, a good pupil. He writes carelessly—it is not just a case of bad proof-reading. His style is repetitious, awkward, slovenly. And that is not all. He is deficient in plain, simple French. In *The Red and the Black* he always says "anti-sympathy." Why not "antipathy"? I could give no end of such examples. His French almost touches the illiterate at times.

And the curious thing is that this accusation, against

which Stendhal finds his defenders, is allowed to be brought against Balzac, who finds far fewer advocates. That is unjust. Balzac scratched and scratched at his proofs, indefinitely. He had a sense of rhythm, and at times some concern about it. The charming passage in *Droll Stories*, where he describes Tours as a beautiful girl bathing her feet in the Loire, might fit any anthology. Esther's letters in *À Combien l'Amour* (by no means one of his best novels) are delightful things delicately balanced. Mistakes in French, actual cases of negligence, are less frequent in him than in Stendhal. But he did not aim at "style." Stylism had not been invented in those days—it dates from Théophile Gautier, then from the Goncourts. Hugo alone, because of his grandiloquence frequently less bearable in his prose than in his verse, remains grammatically impeccable and rhythmically oratorical. But Balzac had a particular conception of the novel. It has sometimes been said that Flaubert wrote a paragraph excellently, a chapter less well, a book badly. That is not true. If ever novel was well written it is assuredly *Madame Bovary*. But the description might be given inversely, and much more justly, of Balzac: he wrote a paragraph loosely, a chapter much better, a book admirably. Knowing what the novel is, what a novel ought to be, he sacrificed everything to total impressions.

In Stendhal the composition is loose, loose in *La Chartreuse de Parme*, loose also in *Le Rouge et le Noir*. Nevertheless, he arrives at total effects by the vital energy, the very life, with which all his work is packed. So thinks Barrès. Voguë regretted that such energy was used "for the worse," but the vitality itself he does not deny; and from the point of view of art, a novelist has the right not to be a moralist, or to be at least an immoral moralist; and the essence, the soul, of Stendhal's work, is his delight in energy and, consequently (again as in Balzac, as in all our fiction), his worship of heroism. He says as much himself in so many words. Remember Mathilde's cry in *Le Rouge et le Noir*: "Is any act truly great without being *extreme* at the moment of accomplishment?" (Italics his.) Naïvely heroic is Fabrice in *La Chartreuse*, always pursuing the grand deed and the difficult conquest in love. Passionately heroic is the Duchess Sanseverina, immoderate in all her acts. Even the sceptic Count Mosca is a romantic Metternich, heroic after his fashion, or rather after the fashion of Stendhal, who overstresses everything. Heroic also the touching Mme. de Rênal in her struggle, where passion and conjugal fidelity clash—a true sister to the Princesse de Clèves and to Mme. de Mortsauf—and much more appealing than the heroine of the *Lily of the Valley*, precisely because she has weakened, precisely because she is not "all of a piece," but a woman, a real woman—a vanquished heroine!

This traditional taste for heroism explains why the writers of the great era of Romanticism felt such great enthusiasm for the "virtue" of the "monsters of the Renaissance." It also explains why their characters are "types"—Goriot, Grandet, Julien Sorel, Mathilde, Mme. de Rênal. They are more than life-sized—you can see them at great distances! A few pages hence we shall be witnessing the progressive agony and final disappearance of "hero" and "heroine," and, as a further consequence, the end of the "type" whose name and face the reader remembers. It may be something like what happened at the end of the golden age of the "romance of chivalry." Heroism is becoming ridiculous. The Don Quixote of our day is named Tartarin!

IX

NATURALISM AND STYLISM

IT MAY seem a paradox to say so—yet not only do Naturalism and Stylism go together, historically, but they are intimately associated. Never the one without the other—the case of the Goncourts!

"My brother's novels and mine," wrote the survivor in 1895, "aimed above all else to put an end to adventure in the novel. One of the peculiar traits of our novels proves that they are the most faithful to history of any novels from this age." (*Journal*, 1861) . . . "The public likes false novels: this novel is a true novel . . . the study that follows is a clinic on love." (*Germinie Lacerteux*, preface, 1865.)

So much for the "Naturalism," which at first was called "Realism." As to style—the two brothers are in search "of an individual style, very personal, very Goncourt." With them this style will be something glittering but blurred, in reaction against the oratorical rhythm of the writers just preceding, "impressionistic," in short, set off by the use of unusual words, archaisms, or by current novelties now invented by them, now borrowed from slang.

Along with the Goncourts Théophile Gautier introduced style into the novel. But he had not "rejected adventure," nor even the fantastic, as witness the *Romance of the Mummy, Captain Fracasse* and even *Mademoiselle de Maupin*. One may note that it is perhaps this attention to style that has prevented those novels of Gautier's from attaining the popularity of *The Three Musketeers* of the elder Dumas, for example. When adventure rather than psychology, the deeper significance of persons and things, constitutes the substance of a work, the reader likes to believe "that it all happened"; and he does not succeed in believing that it all happened if the author asserts himself, thrusts himself forward, is forever "doing stunts" before the reader's eyes. It takes a sorcerer actually to create things, to pull a bird out of a hat, or materialize a ghost; and such feats are sleight-of-hand. "How clever!" we say. An impression fatal to plausibility!

That was the experience of the Goncourts, more even than of Gautier himself. Add to that, moreover, that those two perfect gentlemen of letters seem to have been particularly deficient in a real creative inventiveness. May it not have been by very reason of this lack of imagination that they were so heated in asserting that the novel could and should get on without it? The fact is that nowadays no one reads *Charles Demailly, Sister Philomène, Germinie Lacerteux, Madame Gervaise*; and very few read *Renée Mauperin* and *Manette Salomon*, books still interesting though they fail to thrill. It is none the less true that, by the fervor of their convictions, by their disinterestedness, by their sincere enthusiasm (in spite of petty jealousies) for any work which they considered not only in harmony with their literary credo, but beautiful, really beautiful, they "made a school." So it was in the musical dynasty of the Bachs: it happens at times that the son outshines the father, and virtually extinguishes the father's fame.

This school—style was only one of its dogmas—was inclined to strike an alliance, as regarded prose, with the "art for art group" (art, that is, apart from morality and politics). The Second Empire, at the time in its infancy, tended to favor this movement in a rather adroit fashion, through the agency of Princess Mathilde's salon, which passed—that was the adroitness—as Liberal and "of the Opposition." Let us not forget: from this salon the decree went forth (Saint-Beuve, no less, was the herald to proclaim the bull of excommunication) that Erckmann-Chatrian's novels, on the military disasters which put an end to the First Empire, were *not* literature. In all conscience I could not share that opinion. If Zola's *Débâcle* is literature, as no one doubted when the book first appeared (it is true that the prosecution is still continuing, but without

final judgment as yet), the *Conscript of 1813* is literature also, for it is superior in interest and in soundness to *La Débâcle*, with a "truth to life" which the
latter novel does not have. Read one after the other and
judge for yourself! But Erckmann and Chatrian were
republicans, as were almost all Alsatians at that time.
Had they been Bonapartists, the judgment issuing from
the Princess Mathilde's salon would, without doubt,
have been quite different. And this provokes an aside
in my mind, as to the present-day dictatorships in
Italy, Spain, Russia and Poland. Instead of enforcing a
brutal censorship which strangles without guiding, why
do they not use a more delicate touch and prompt the
formation of little circles like the Princess Mathilde's
—anti-political in appearances, and even "of the Opposition"—but what a charming and benevolent, and,
one may say, effective, Opposition?

We must of course bear in mind that if the doctrine
that it is the artist's duty to hold aloof from politics
was practised by the Goncourt brothers, it was not so
faithfully respected by their immediate disciples, or by
those whom they considered such (Flaubert excepted
perhaps. Though deeply stirred by the German victory
of 1870, Flaubert on the whole remained inaccessible
to everything not strictly pertaining to his art). The
writers of the Second Empire were as much inclined

to be hostile to the absolutism of the government—to be republican, as many literary men of today are to show their contempt or their distrust for parliamentary democracy. It may simply be that young men love opposition. There may also be deeper reasons for the situation. For the moment, let us keep to one fact: at that time there was a "myth" of the Republic and a mystical Republicanism, just as in our day there is a mystical neo-monarchism, and a myth of Monarchy and Legitimacy.

For politically minded people who read Joseph de Maistre with as much pleasure as Proudhon—Ah! what a natively artistic nation is France, and what a joy to stumble on a Proudhon, after all the gibberish of a Karl Marx! But for artistic minds who, as regards religion, find as much satisfaction in the crude blasphemies of Mme. Ackermann as in the mystical effusions of Verlaine, who enjoy all colors, providing the colors make a pretty picture, changes in the political front are interesting only in so far as art is concerned. And in that case we are obliged to note that republican, democratic, or, if you wish, parliamentary opinions, have colored the work of Alphonse Daudet and given it a peculiar tone, a peculiar temper; just as the opposite opinions may be lending a peculiar tone, a peculiar temper, to the writings of the present generation. In my eyes the one set of opinions is as important, or as un-important, as the other. What counts is the artistic result.

It is a fact not without its force that as a matter of political, humanitarian faith, as a matter of tempera-ment and of native kindness of heart, Alphonse Dau-det turned toward the sorrows and unhappy conditions of life, not of the peasants and the working classes—these he did not know at first hand (he came from "small property" in a country town), but of his own people, the small-town business classes. That fact, along with the influence of Dickens, visible not only in his sentimentality in general, but in secondary char-acters such as Délobelle, the actor without a job, gave us *Fromont Junior and Risler Senior*, a delightful novel.

It is also a fact not without its force that this same humanitarian and republican mysticism affected Zola. If the Republic, which "was so beautiful under the Empire" and still looked so on its first public appear-ances to those who had acclaimed its birth, triumph-antly enforced our just laws, there would be no more prostitutes like Nana, no more disgusting and vicious *bourgeois* like Pot-Bouille; and *Germinal* proclaimed, in the face of cruelties for which a soulless capitalism was responsible, better days for the poor workers in the coal mines. We can readily understand how Zola came to throw himself with the violence and impulsiveness so well remembered into the Dreyfus affair. It was not at all, as his enemies charged, that he sought notoriety. He had plenty of notoriety already. The truth was that in view of his temperament, everything he ever did had a publicity value. He believed, sincerely, in all the great dreams—all the "bunk," if you wish—of the heroic age of '48: justice, and truth, which he believed materially, scientifically, demonstrable—an ingenuousness to be detected in Taine, though Taine's lightness of touch was lacking to the heavier, much more lumbering, mind of Zola.

Zola knows no nuances; he is crude, he is gross—I am not thinking so much of his "obscenities." Writers have now gone so far, there has been so much refining, in the vicious direction, since Zola's time, that his obscenity looks like innocence itself—it is a matter of words, not of things. I am speaking rather of his vulgarity. Zola's style is vulgar. And yet—something very characteristic of the Goncourt school—he did his best to have one. Zola, too, aspired to artistry: imitation goods, never the real thing, an article for the bargain counter, bombast, fireworks, "fine writing!" I must have been about the first to say, away back in 1890, that Zola was to be placed, in a literary sense, at the confluence of Balzac and Hugo. My remark has been frequently repeated since. As I think it over now, I am inclined to feel that the Hugo current holds a greater place in Zola's work than the Balzac current. In Balzac, observation is direct, living—it is "re-creation." In Zola, it is veneer, without feeling—nothing more than documentation (another defect of the Goncourts). And then there is his materialism, his materialistic philosophy, no less vulgar, and a little colored, in some novels, by a pessimism derived from Schopenhauer, whose influence was active at the time Zola was writing. Is that too just fustian? And yet it is all truth! It is "formidably" true, to use one of Zola's favorite adverbs. It is a truth by virtue of that very Romanticism, of which one of his characters complains "that his generation is sunk in it up to the belly, in spite of all efforts to extricate itself."

With eyes only for physiological man and physiological woman, looking at them from below, as it were, in terms of environment or in terms of a physical mechanism hardly more complex than that of their four-legged brothers and sisters, "their heredity having laws as fixed as gravity," he exaggerates them perforce. He exaggerates them by the very brilliance with which he paints his backgrounds, by the heavy but at the same time oratorical and lyric movement of this made-to-order style, so vigorous in spite of everything. Zola is pathetic, he is sentimental, but in all sincerity. (Re-read little Lalie's death in *L'Assommoir*.) In a word, what with qualities and defects, Zola has everything that people do not have today and are doing their best not to have. Said René Lalou not long since in his *History of Contemporary Literature*: "Most of Zola's books are (today) completely neglected by the public." But some two weeks ago I happened to be talking with a publisher and he said: "Zola is picking up again. It is something quite noticeable." These two contrary estimates from the business point of view may perhaps be reconciled. Go to the retailers of the fashionable quarters in Paris and you will find no Zola in the show windows, and hardly any on the shelves. But turn to the more populous districts and you will find two or three volumes in the windows. This is what has happened: Zola portrayed a certain middle class and worked for it. That class exists no longer. It has grown educated, it has grown wealthy, in spite of the hard times brought on by the War. It has changed its ideas and its manners of living. But the masses meantime have been making money too. They are living today the way people of moderate prosperity were living in Zola's time. They have adopted those aspirations, those jealousies, those habits of mind. They are finding themselves, or perhaps are trying to find themselves, in Zola.

Zola was an author of universal suffrage. That is his merit and his defect. He always wanted to be great, or rather monstrous. He succeeded in being monstrous rather than great. Some of his minor characters, Mouquette, for instance, and Bazouge, the grave-digger, will live. He left only one type: Coupeau, the "bum."

Alphonse Daudet likewise, as I have said, bequeaths only one type to posterity: Tartarin. Shall I dare confess that for the Tartarin series as a whole, and even for the first, the authentic, the only, Tartarin, the *Tartarin de Tarascon*, I share the general esteem only half-heartedly? The character is conceived from without, not from within. It is a caricature of our Southerner, not a portrait. As for psychology, none at all, or, at the most, a very elementary one! The single original thing in the work is to have mingled Don Quixote and Sancho Panza in one person, Tartarin. And even that is not striking enough. It is amusing, nothing more.

But the man himself was charming and one feels the man in his books without offense. He was affected by the pessimism of the Naturalists. In *Numa Roumestan, The Nabob, Kings in Exile, Sappho, The Evangelist*, his best novels, the unhappy ending is obligatory; but one feels that he yields to such gloom just as he yields to his "notes," his "documents," somewhat against his will. He is gay, he is sensitive, superficially but truly. In spite of the doctrine of his school, which forced pessimism upon him, he is an out-and-out optimist. People have pretended, in view of that, that he was of Jewish descent: Daudet would be a contraction of "Davidet," "little David," the "son of David"—and optimism is a Jewish trait! All this is a plain fairy story, cooked up to torment his son, Léon Daudet. In Provence and Languedoc there are many Davids, Protestant or even Catholic, in whose veins not a drop of Jewish blood has ever flowed. Let us take Alphonse Daudet for what he really was, a descendant of small-town business people of the South, who, for generations, had found life modest, sweet, pleasant and happy, even in semi-poverty. People never take anything very seriously there; they are easily moved to tears; they even more easily dry them. Daudet comes naturally by his charm, and even more naturally by his good nature. He is a pocket edition of Dickens, more of a poet but less vigorous. It is not surprising that his work should be occasionally reminiscent of the *Pickwick Papers* and *David Copperfield*. He felt quite at home in the work of the great Englishman. He came from a province where, as in the England of 1830, life, especially rural and business life, was easy even for people of moderate means. That is why the part of his work that is most "Southern," *Letters from my Mill* and *Numa Roumestan*, appear to us the truer, the more sincere, the more enduring.

X

FLAUBERT AND MAUPASSANT

NO ONE, surely, would go to such lengths of absurdity as to suggest that Flaubert was produced by the Goncourts—the dates would be against it! The truth is that in their fight for style, the Goncourts regarded Flaubert as an ally and an example— an example, if not a model. There is, in fact, nothing in common between the impressionistic, visual style of the Goncourts, made up of little touches, little spots, as it were, cleverly fitted together into a mosaic, and the oratorical, cadenced, preferably lyrical style of Flaubert, which, though stamped all over with his temperament and his genius, shows traces not only of Chateaubriand but of Bossuet. . . . Just recall, in the admirable finale of *Madame Bovary*, the passage where the woman who is dying of poison receives extreme unction: the priest applies the holy ointment to her forehead, her eyes, her mouth, her hands, and her feet—to feet "wont of yore to trip so lightly to the gratifiance of her desires, but destined now to walk no further." Does this not remind one of some beautiful flight in the *Funeral Orations*? In the French not a rare, dazzling or scintillating word, such as the Goncourts would have used: just plain, every-day, modern French! Then suddenly

you encounter a strange term of an antique cast—
"gratifiance" *assouvissance*, in place of the ordinary
word *assouvissement*, "gratification." Church preachers
in France have actually adopted the word!

The influence of Bossuet—but the influence also of
Chateaubriand, the Chateaubriand of *Atala*, the magnificent Chateaubriand of *Memories from Beyond the
Tomb*; and the influence furthermore of Romanticism,
the grand strophe turned into prose, that Hugo uses:
grandiose and, I will even say, grandiloquent. . . .
In *Salammbô*, for instance: "Have you seen her great
eyes, under those great eyebrows, like suns beneath
triumphal arches? . . . Every evening, remember, she
goes up to the roof-top of her palace. Ah! the very
stones must tremble under her sandals, and the stars
lean down to gaze at her!" And further in *Salammbô*,
where the mercenaries are condemned to kill each
other: "A common lot had formed deep affections
among the men. Camp, for most of them, took the
place of home and country. Living without families,
they vented their needs of tenderness upon their com-
rades, and they would fall asleep in the starlight,
side by side, under the same cloaks. . . . In those perpetual wanderings, in the course of countless battles,
murders, adventures, strange loves had been formed,
obscene unions as earnest as marriages, wherein the

elder defended the younger in battle, cooled feverish lips on his brow, stole forage to feed him. And the other, a child picked up on the side of a road and become a mercenary, would repay such thoughtful attentions by wifely devotions. . . . They exchanged their jewelled collars and earrings, gifts which they had made each other in days gone by at moments of danger or intoxicated joy. All begged to die. But no one would strike the blow! Here and there a youth would say to another warrior whose beard was gray: 'No, no, you are the stronger—you will avenge us! Kill me!' And the other: 'I have fewer years to live: strike, never mind—at my heart!' They pulled open their mailed shirts that the sword points might pierce more quickly. The deep stripes on their skins from the lashes they received at Carthage *were like so many inscriptions on so many columns*."

The simile is overstrong, exaggerated, improbable —like many of Barbey d'Aurevilly's images—but it is unforgettable, it is tremendous. And it was in this admirable flight of cadenced prose that for the first time, to my knowledge, what has since been called "Corydonism" made its appearance in contemporary French literature (strange that André Gide never thought of that!).

In Flaubert, therefore, we have a tenacious survival

of Romantic traditions. Furthermore, his Norman origins (law-suits, courts, prosecutions, pleadings, appeals) incline him to the oratorical style—the same trait that appears in Corneille, and in the Algerian essays of a Norman unjustly forgotten: Masquery. But there is also the influence of the Goncourt school, with which Flaubert is in close touch, which considers him a powerful ally and a great master, and which he respects, in his turn, because of its contempt for slovenly writing and its worship of style. These two currents mingle in two masterpieces, *Madame Bovary* and *l'Éducation Sentimentale*; the pessimistic realism of the Goncourt school holds the field alone in *Bouvard et Pécuchet*; Romanticism, concentrated, compact (and all the more violent, for that reason) in *Salammbô*, the three successive stages of *The Temptation of Saint Anthony*, and the first two of the Three Short Stories, *Herodias*, and *Saint Julien, the Hospitaler*. And is Romanticism entirely absent from *Bouvard et Pécuchet*? Flaubert feels an uncontrollable need of drawing "great good men" more than life-sized, even in their foolishness. The same need breaks in upon the character of Emma Bovary—an overdrawing of sentiment vitiated to sentimentality; in the immortal Homais—an overdrawing of unimaginative stupidity; in Mathô, of *Salammbô*, an overdrawing of primitive, animal passion.

Even Hamilcar, a secondary character in *Salammbô*, strikes heroic, theatrical attitudes—poses from the stage of the grand era of Romanticism and even of the melodrama. Hamilcar rises before the council of Carthage, which is accusing his daughter of having been Mathô's mistress and given him the "Zaimph": "By the hundred torches of your intelligence, by . . ." (and here five lines of sonorous apostrophe) "I swear that you have lied in accusing my daughter." Then in a lower tone: ". . . and I shall not even speak to her about it!" Bouvard and Pécuchet are heroic by dint of sheer ineptitude—no one, in reality, has ever been so stupid. They are superhuman by dint of being too sub-human; and so is Homais, by dint of being himself and nothing else. That is why Bouvard, Pécuchet, and especially Homais are, perhaps, with Tartarin, the last "types" created by our literature. They are ridiculous, as I said, just as Don Quixote is ridiculous. People refuse to take grandeur seriously any longer, or else they will accept grandeur only in lunatics. The generations following Flaubert will gradually replace portraits of general types with studies of exceptional cases.

But there is still Emma Bovary, herself, an eternal type; so much so that Louis Bertrand was able very properly to contribute to our language the word "bovarysm" to denote a certain kind of mind, a sentimental, unreal attitude towards life quite commonly found in women and even in some men. May one not say, for example, that General Boulanger, a political leader, in killing himself on the grave of a mistress he could not live without, was touched with "bovarysm"? Emma is the eternal, the universal, type of the amorous, romantic woman, who mingles the vulgar and the humdrum with a touching need of love. It is very possible that, to Flaubert, on first thought, she may have appeared ridiculous. But that would be the case also with Cervantes and Don Quixote, and with Dickens and Pickwick—that absurd Pickwick who, in the opinion of Sam Weller, ends by becoming "an angel in short breeches and buckled shoes." It is humanly impossible for an author to dig deeply into a character in order to pack him with all the traits he can possess, and then not end by loving him. A woman dying for love is never ridiculous! That is why, through its powerful creation of a universal type, *Madame Bovary* has not only become one of the greatest French novels of the Nineteenth century, but has had echoes throughout European literature.

English literature as well as the others! Mr. Ford Madox Ford admits as much, generously, and even with pleasure. And I can cite an example that he does not give. In Shanghai one day a man bought a cheap

English novel which he thought was a new book. The title was unknown to him and so was the name of the author. He opened it. It was a piracy of *Madame Bovary*, doubtless intended for the Chinese who read English but also, I imagine, for a goodly number of Englishmen. So *Madame Bovary* became part of the public domain before the legal term—the domain of our common humanity, that is!

With the name of Flaubert, critics frequently associate the name of Guy de Maupassant who was, however (whatever may have been said on the point), neither his nephew, nor his god-son, but just, in the early days, his most faithful disciple. It is well to bear this in mind: in making Maupassant share in his researches and help in the documentation of *Bouvard et Pécuchet*, in making him "go and study a tree until it seemed to him different from all other trees," Flaubert was his teacher and gave him his start, clearing his mind of rubbish, guiding him, training him. But the pupil had a personality of his own. There are no rhetorical sentences, or very few, in Maupassant. There is no imitation of the Goncourts. In 1888, when he had fully developed, he rises in his wrath against the "cluttered, complicated Chinese vocabulary that is being imposed on us today in the name of style." He had a limpid style, on the contrary, employing only the most

usual words; we might even call it thin, did we not
sense, at the first glance, that it is a sinewy thing after
the very manner of the half vulgar Norman himself,
whom one of his numerous mistresses described as a
"sad-faced bull."

"A very gifted story-teller, a very charming anec-
dotist!" said Edmond de Goncourt of him in 1892.
"But a stylist? A great writer? No, no!"

Retaining at least the first part of this jealous judgment, people as a rule try to make Maupassant the
greatest short-story writer of the Nineteenth century,
the best, the foremost. They forget that another sur-
passed him in merit and in significance: Anatole France.
I shall return to this subject farther along to substan-
tiate my estimate. Meanwhile, let us remember that the
author of *Bel-Ami, Mont-Oriol, Pierre et Jean, Fort
Comme la Mort*, and *Notre Coeur*, was also a fairly
great and powerful novelist. The truth is, nevertheless,
that if we still read Maupassant, it is as a short-story
writer. A mistake, perhaps, but such is the fact! As
a short-story writer, he wielded an influence so strong,
so lasting, that it has overstepped the borders of French
literature and gone as far abroad as Russia—Tchekhof,
for example. And all this, for certain reasons, is understandable enough. Taine reproved him mildly, in a
letter he wrote in 1882, for dealing only with peasants,

small-town people, students, prostitutes. "Some day, doubtless" (the "doubtless" was merely a courteous attenuation), "you will get around to a few cultivated people, the upper *bourgeoisie* . . . To my mind civilization is also a power."

There is some truth in what Taine says. One cannot evade the facts: the great writer is the man who, as Balzac did, gives us a society whole, who can go from the bottom up as well as from the top down. Nevertheless, one should also remember this: it was just because Maupassant, at least the Maupassant of the first manner, the manner of the short stories, painted only working people, peasants, small-town people, prostitutes, that this part of his work still retains a present-day interest in our country, and has had such success abroad. Peasants, workingmen, prostitutes, small-town people—they are the ones who change least, and least quickly, and are least affected by external developments in civilization. Another thing: because they are least responsive to external pressures, one may go to them as to the backward or savage peoples, to find the instincts and passions of humanity surviving in their elementary, primitive forms. That is why *La Maison Tellier,* or *Les Contes de la Bécasse,* can be understood in Russia and even in China (where they have just been translated) as readily as in France. On the same score—though at a slightly higher level—the Annamites crowd into performances of Molière's comedies, transferred into their language, whereas they would never translate Henri Bataille. In the Seventeenth century French conceptions of the family and of social rankings were not far different from those prevailing in the Orient today. Institutions have changed with us, not with the Chinese.

Furthermore, while attaining to perfect art through their very condensations, their simplifications, their suppressions of useless details, the short stories of Maupassant revert to the exquisitely French tradition of the *fabliaux*, and may therefore be considered as popular art, "folk-art," in the best sense of the term.

But Maupassant evolved. *Notre Coeur, Pierre et Jean, Fort Comme la Mort*, are novels, psychological novels, novels about "civilized people," as Taine's letter desired. There may be two factors in his development. For one thing, his success, or rather his successes, literary and feminine, the ones entailing the others, had brought him into contact with "civilized people," into "society": whereof he was not a little proud and could brag that he knew the *Almanach de Gotha* by heart. In the second place he was already suffering from the consequences of the same disease that destroyed Baudelaire, Nietzsche, and Jack London. In artists and men of imagination, it happens that the early symptoms of those ravages which are destined one day to plunge them into unending gloom at first produce a strange exhilaration of happiness. They see another world with a subtle intensity. They become different men. So, in one night, a great fire may glow with wondrous brilliancy only to show ashes and ruins at dawn. I do not care to dwell on the relations of disease and talent. I merely suggest that to some such thing we owe the heartrending insight—withal so resolutely expressed— of Maupassant's *Notre Coeur*.

> Give me, oh Lord, the strength, the courage give,
> To view my body and my heart without disgust!

Such the cry of Baudelaire. And one seems to hear an echo of it in the supreme creations of Maupassant. And if that diseased second-sight which suddenly came to him has served to give us *just that*, the fact would be more interesting to note than the undisputed influence of progressive disease on certain of his fantastic tales, such as *Horla*.

XI

THE "SOCIETY" NOVEL

"SOCIETY," or rather, a certain section of society, respectable people, right-thinking, living in deference to certain conventions, believing that society, as society is organized (very much to their advantage) is perfect, or nearly so, and that it should remain as it is, just as the Nineteenth century made it . . . There is a whole literature for such people!

Ford Madox Ford, in this connection, distinguishes between the "novel," the real "novel," and the "nuvvel," a term he coins to denote a work of the imagination which is also respectful of the conventions in question, and flatters the vanities of certain people of wealth, just below the aristocracy, who incline toward ultra-conservatism, are convinced of the sacro-sanctity of their rights, and are grimly determined that a cat shall not be called a cat and that fundamentals shall never be discussed. An air of commercialism hangs about the "nuvvel." It is always artificial, always strongly "society."

Mr. Ford outlines the general scheme of such a story. His formula may be a trifle mischievous. It is, at any rate, amusing and true. In a novel of this kind you will invariably "see an English Manor House inhabited by the Best People: Sir Thomas, amiable, but not bright; Lady Charlotte, benevolent, charitable—an Earl's daughter; Misses Jean and Charlotte, pure as dew within lily-chalices; Mister Tom, not absolutely satisfactory, though he will some day be so; Mister Edward, always satisfactory; pigeons, a rose garden, a corps of domestics stiff and well-trained; a rectory with its Episcopal clergyman! And you will see a whole countryside, a whole continent, so conducted that these amiable but not bright personages shall lead amiable, idle and almost blameless existences of their own choice in an atmosphere of courtesy and cap-touchings." So did a society well satisfied with itself conceive "good literature," "healthy literature," in the Victorian era; and "from England to the Government of Kiev, from the State of Massachusetts to the Department of the Var, you found households modelling themselves upon it."

In the Department of the Var? Say rather, in the whole of France! For we had that literature also, and we still have it: it is Octave Feuillet; it is, up to a certain point, Cherbuliez. The *Revue des Deux Mondes*, which, in its day, published the novels of George Sand, owes it to itself and to its readers to publish novels of that kind, novels which pay deference to morality, and show Army officers, priests, proprietors, financiers and

manufacturers acting in attractive rôles. Not that they
do not fall into certain errors, succumb on occasion to
blameworthy passions, or dally with them at least. But
never in the way ordinary mortals do! The late Gaston
Calmette once said to a writer: "Send me a novel for
Figaro: a good clean book—you know, a little adultery, but fashionable!"

Even the novels of Paul Bourget fall into this *genre*,
just as, according to Mr. Ford, the novels of Thack-
eray and Dickens do, across the Channel. For the "nuvvel" does not preclude talent, even talent of the high-
est order. One will never understand anything about
anything in France, whether in politics or literature,
unless one bears in mind that we have "provinces,"
and that "the provinces" (thank Heaven—at least
from the point of view of social conservation and sta-
bility of ideals and morals!) cling to a certain reserve,
a certain shyness (a certain hypocrisy, if one will have
it so). Human passions may be the same in town and
country, but they are not discussed in the country the
way they are in Paris, nor is it the same *bourgeoisie*,
nor the same aristocracy, that peep into books. Reread,
if you have time, Octave Feuillet's *Sybille*—a blood relation of Madame Bovary. But Feuillet's Emma has a
noble title, instead of being a farmer's daughter, wife
to a druggist. She lives in a château with a park around

it—and she rides, not in a hired cab, but on the back of a swan!

Of course, there are people in the small towns, young men, students, girls, who read something else, something fresher, more piquant, less conventional. But keep to the "settled" people: they think it owing to their station in life to stick to such novels, and they try to make the conventions of that fiction the realities of their lives. Indeed, the circumstances and considerations whereby convention, or the necessary social deferences, actually become realities for individuals, would itself make a fine subject for a true and beautiful novel—a subject worthy of a Julian Green, for example, who has just brought to our French literature a capacity for exactitude in detail, and a ferocity in pessimistic observation, which one would be tempted to call Anglo-Saxon, had we not already had *Bouvard et Pécuchet*, and other French realists of much less merit and significance. There is something religious, something Calvinistic, about Green, who is, by the way, a Catholic, though certainly reared in a Protestant environment. His religious feeling might be translated thus: men and women live forever under the curse that drove them from the Garden of Eden; they are not made to be happy in this world!

I cannot bring myself to condemn beyond appeal the

"society" novel of a pious turn. The piety is false, sometimes, but not always! There is evident sincerity in the books of Henri Bordeaux, for instance, which almost always deal with provincial life (Savoy). Not only in the case of Bordeaux, but also, and for still stronger reasons, in the case of Paul Bourget, such novels fill the needs (shall I say the legitimate needs?) of a fairly large group of readers. But once they prove successful, as does not always happen with authors of lesser talent, who exploit the *genre* for money-making purposes, the demands of the same readers compel them to maintain (as is notably the case with Cherbuliez) careful concern for good writing and for good plots—plots, that is, capable of interesting the average reader.

On the whole, however, this somewhat hybrid brand of fiction had never attained in France the importance it has in Anglo-Saxon literature; doubtless because strictly literary taste is more assertive and more widely spread among us than among our neighbors, and because the judgments artists and writers pass upon each other have greater weight with the public at large. On the other hand, the same circumstances have brought about the depreciation, in the eyes of French authors and French artists, of the "novel of adventure." This is regarded as a non-literary type, and the greatest contempt is visited upon the masterpiece of the *genre*, the *Three Musketeers* of the elder Dumas.

Such contempt is both unjust and dangerous. As for the injustice—if the Iliad is not a novel of warlike adventure in verse, and the Odyssey a novel of maritime adventure in verse, what are they? And the immortal *Robinson Crusoe*—it is, or is it not, a literary masterpiece? And the *Chartreuse de Parme*, is it, or is it not, full of conspiracies, escapes, and fortresses—towers a hundred feet high, whence the hero makes his way to freedom with the help of the jailer's daughter? It need not be said that but for the *Three Musketeers* we should never had the *Soldiers Three* of Kipling. These Englishmen are greater, and truer to life, than their French ancestors; but is that not all the more reason for leaving a place for those ancestors in the history of our literature?

Finally, I must remark, this most unfortunate contempt may be partly responsible for the failure of our contemporary letters to show the equivalent of a Jack London or a Conrad. Pierre Benoît might have become at least a second Cherbuliez (compare *Koenigsmark* with *Comte Kostia*). But he has been thrust, as it were by force, into the ambiguous *genre* of the quasi-popular, though "distinguished," novel. He tried to escape from it in *Mademoiselle de la Ferté*, and in *Atilke* (both noteworthy books) and in *Erromango*. But the special audience which had been virtually imposed upon him failed to follow his new lead. This divorce, made necessary by his increasing intellectuality, and his too faithful regard for one of the dogmas of the Goncourt school, is something to be regretted. It amounts to excommunicating not only adventure, but imagination itself!

XII

LOTI AND EXOTICISM

AND yet—we have had Loti! Loti is just a miracle! But since there are people who do not believe in miracles, I will state a few facts.

Loti has no "imagination," the moment we take the term in its current acceptation as "inventiveness," "plot-making." But he has all the imagination in the world, if the word be taken in its original sense—a capacity for expressing images and recalling memories of images. Fiction, composition, invention? No trace of any! Just return to the best of his novels, *My Brother Ives*. Nothing happens, absolutely nothing! A Breton mariner goes to sea "on shares." He has a good heart, but bad judgment. He is addicted to drink—an abominable drunkard, in fact. He repents, starts life over again, takes a wife. Her character is barely sketched; we have little to do with her; she has no adventures, either. As for Ives, there is no excitement in his life—not even a shipwreck. There is no "action." In the end he reforms again, and will drink no more! That is the whole story.

Loti's Marriage is a sequence of little notes, thrown together haphazard, on Tahiti about the year 1872, when that Cytherean isle still retained something of what Bougainville had seen there before the double contact with China on the one hand, and Europe and America on the other, had wrought devastation everywhere. And—nothing happens! Bathing in the sea, singing and lovemaking under the palms, sketches of Queen Pomaré and her family, men who are wild and blood-thirsty giants, girls who are pathetic little things with tuberculosis . . . It is a superb race that feels it is dying and is not afraid of death; though it is afraid of the dead and is fascinated by them. There is a little Tahitian girl, Rarahu, a mere child, who plays now with life and now with her French lover, as she plays with the kitten she owns. She dies, just as Aziyadé, in the book of that name, dies. That is the most notable "episode" in the two novels. And we may say the same of *Madame Chrysanthème, Ramuntcho, Pêcheurs d'Islande.*

Loti's women? They are all dolls, playthings, who never complain of being taken for such: submissiveness, desire, voluptuousness—those the qualities which Loti admires and loves in them. Primitive loves, without deep complications: no "psychology!" A suggestion of philosophical pantheism of a gloomy turn, as in Leconte de Lisle, but in a different spirit, much less haughty and much more afraid. Loti seems as little interested in the "motives" of his characters as he is in what (the nothing) they do. In this he stands at the antipodes of Marcel Proust. It would be hard to conceive a subjectivism more thoroughgoing than his. All nature, from one end of the world to the other, spreads out before him, but really, in spite of the limpid transparency of his style, only as a dream. If the dreamer should vanish, there would be nothing left, no world! And the dreamer *knows* (I underline the word) that he is destined to vanish; whence his anguish in the presence of inevitable death. Loti was a much more perfect egoist than Barrès. If the fact has not been generally remarked, it is because Loti never says so—he suggests it rather, by inference only, and involuntarily at that.

Involuntarily—that is to say: without will—will-less! That is one of the elements in Loti's magic. Never a greater magician than he! Nothing, as I said, in *My Brother Ives*, in *Loti's Marriage, Madame Chrysanthème, Aziyadé*! And yet, it is all admirable, poignant, deeply stirring, unforgettable—magical! Loti is the sorcerer, the true sorcerer, of our literature. There is no sleight-of-hand, no verbal acrobatics, no literary fakirism. The man, as a man, in flesh and bone, rather effeminate, and a little flat, may have had his little coquetries, his little poses. But there is no trace of any such in his work. He was a born writer, a born artist, writing a language utterly smooth and utterly simple, without an artifice. Not that he ever tried to write that way! At the very most, one may note in him a peculiar stylistic procedure. He seems deliberately to use general and apparently commonplace epithets to characterize details that are unusual, striking, or very individual; whereas he keeps his (very rare) surprises for things that are in themselves commonplace or platitudinous. This is just the reverse of the technique prevailing among our present-day writers, who hunt out the shrillest and most striking epithets for everything possible, whether particular or general.

In Loti's work, from one end to the other, I doubt whether a single word may be found which does not belong to the plainest of everyday conversation. Save that—I beg my reader's close attention to the point— he is a musician! A musician in the two senses of the word, the proper and the derived. As for the proper: Loti was not a little proud of his talents as a pianist. As for the derived: all his paragraphs are delicately cadenced strophes, strophes of exquisitely pretty love-songs, as the love song was conceived under the Second Empire and during the early days of the Third Republic, the period of Loti's infancy and youth, so marvelously fraught with sentiment. Certain musical paragraphs of Gounod's *Vallon*, which is a masterpiece of its kind (the words are by Lamartine), breathe a sentiment compounded of an expectation of death and a sort of melancholy intoxication in the presence of Nature. From his earliest youth, writes Loti of himself, he was haunted by a wistful yearning for distant lands bathed in sunlight, *other* lands. He would study such inadequate drawings as tried to portray them. What was his enchantment in such images? This is what he says of it in *Loti's Marriage.* He is sitting at the piano at Queen Pomaré's: "The selection we chose was the one where Vasco, in his *Africaine*, is walking, drunk with emotion, over the isle he has just discovered, a piece of music in which the master has displayed most perfectly all he knew by intuition of the faraway splendors of a land of sunlight and green:

> *Pays merveilleux,*
> *Jardins fortunés,*
> *O Paradis, sorti de l'onde . . ."*

So, in Loti's ear, all his visions and sensations, all his vast, boundless sensitiveness, sang their song, verbally and in music, the song people of his time sang in the romances of Gounod, the famous ballad of Madame de Rothschild (so close to the pretty melodies of the Eighteenth century), or in the great romances, in the duos, and the quintets, of the *Africaine*, which was then considered a masterpiece (and a century or two hence, may be so regarded again—you never can tell!). In any event, one cannot over-emphasize the reactions of the arts one upon the other. The authors of our day, who are obsessed with the syncopes of jazz and "division-ist" music, cannot write the way those of an older day wrote with nothing better to charm their ears than the "four-square" music of our grandfathers. The Symbolists were Wagnerians! And as for the future, which of the arts is going to take the lead over the others to bring on something really new? Will it be music, painting, literature? . . .

However that question may be answered, we have had the miracle, Loti's miracle: *exoticism without adventure*, which spared him the reproaches which certain critics, and especially the liegemen of Goncourtism, would doubtless have had for him; and, in spite of no "plot," no "adventure," by the sheer magic of a sensitiveness that magnifies everything—success, a huge success—glory!

Adventure, passion, an epic note, "action in exoticism," will reappear in Claude Farrère's *Civilisés*, his *Bataille*, his *Homme qui assassina*. Farrère is a rough, vigorous, energetic talent, just the reverse, in manner, of Loti, whom, for that matter, Farrère worships. But it may be that, congenitally, the French find it difficult to think of action and adventure as literature; and in the later work of Claude Farrère (of whose *Opium*

Vapors Pierre Louys said: "What may one not expect from a young man capable of drawing such pictures?") adventure and melodrama set the pace.

Yet different as they are in temperament, Farrère and Loti have one strange thing in common. They are "exoticists," but "anti-colonialists," and especially "anti-civilizationists." They both bestow their sympathy and admiration upon civilizations that do not progress—those of Islam and China (before the recent revolutions). Speaking of Indo-China, Farrère foresees and hails the day "when the pale-faced conquerors will pack up their kits and get out"—something poles removed from Anglo-Saxon notions, from those of Kipling, Conrad, Jack London, who not only regard colonization by the whites as an inevitable fact, but consider the white race superior and rightfully appointed to rule. The difference in attitude may perhaps be a distant echo in French sentiments of Rousseau's influence, an instinctive feeling that the savage "has the right idea of things," and the abiding doctrine of the Revolution that "all men are equal."

The point is always, always, overlooked, but here it is: Loti and Farrère are "exoticists," whereas our real novelist of the "colonial" spirit is Louis Bertrand. Never mind *Mademoiselle de Jessaincourt*, and a few other books of more or less "metropolitan" character.

Forget, for the moment, his scholarly essay on Flaubert, and his impartial and generous devotedness in editing and annotating that giant. Forget, further, his critical and historical studies, and the religious spirit of his *Saint Augustine.* All that aside, and, moreover, it is not fiction—Louis Bertrand is essentially the novelist of Algeria, the writer who has first and best managed to describe Algeria just as it is—a development of tremendous significance in contemporary history, the "melting-pot" wherein twelve hundred thousand Europeans of Latin race—French, Italians, Spaniards, and fourteen hundred thousand if we add Morocco and Tunis—are being smelted into a new race—: a sort of "white America" which this time is Latin, whereas the former is Germanic and Saxon.

Blood of the Races forces this fact brilliantly upon the eye and upon the mind, a tough, vigorous, living story. *Pepète le Bien-aimé* is almost as good, with its effervescences and crudities which connect it with certain of the old Spanish novels, on the one hand, and with our Sixteenth century on the other. I venture to confess that I like this book much better than Daudet's *Tartarin.* North Africa has recognized Louis Bertrand as her spiritual father, the man who placed her on the literary map. And that is plain justice. When Louis Bertrand became publicly a Catholic, I suspected that his enthusiastic approval of Latin achievements in North Africa had something to do with it. In his eyes those lands are a Roman and Christian, not a Mohammedan, country. We are the historic heirs of the civilizing imperialism of Rome! Islam is the accident! Doubtless Bertrand dreams, like Father de Foucaud, of baptizing all the Mussulmans. Islamic local color? The facile exoticism of the *burnous*? Nothing of it! Laziness, and fat! He says so bluntly and courageously in *Oriental Mirage*—not a novel, a pamphlet rather, for Bertrand likes an argument; and, strangely enough, in this, he is picking up again a contention long sustained by Gobinau.

One can only share Bertrand's opinion as to the importance, over a century past, of the Franco-Europeanization of North Africa, and the still greater importance it is going to have. Of the rest one may doubt, and keep for Islam the kindly feelings of Loti and Farrère, which are not entirely absent in Chevrillon. One may question whether Islam is only an accident in North Africa. If accident it be, it is an accident of a thousand years' standing! And why did Christianity vanish from the land of Saint Augustine and Saint Jerome, while Judaism held its ground? There may be more deeply seated reasons for such things than Bertrand explains in his *Saint Augustine.* Not that, in this African volume, which the author continues in his *Sanguis Martyrum* (a novel), there is not a world of ardor, faith, and energy, a strength that floods it with life!

XIII

ANATOLE FRANCE

OVER a period of twenty years the great man honored me with his friendship. I owe him the most inspiring lessons, if not in art—his was inimitable—at least in freedom of judgment; for no man was ever freer in thought—he has even been accused of "intellectual anarchism." In dealing with a memory so dear to me, I shall try to forget that friendship and hold to an unbiased view of Anatole France.

"I wish I could own a pretty garden, and live on the edge of the forest." So spake Sylvestre Bonnard. It is perhaps the single allusion to Nature in all of France's work, and it is the allusion a "man of the towns" would make. I remember that one day I told Anatole France that I was leaving for Corsica. "What in the world are you going to do down there?" he cried. "There's not a thing to see!" He meant: not a monument, not a work of art, the only things in the world that interested him at all keenly, along with conversation with people, social life, politics. Your true townsman, your real "citizen"!

To be more precise, a "petty-bourgeois" Parisian, quite as such people were under the Second Empire, the days when France was a boy. Pray do not give the term the wrong slant! From our Seventeenth century on, our great men of letters have come, almost all, from the poorer business classes; and what greater proof of our high grade of civilization than that such men can attain supremest cultivation in tastes, talents, intelligence? France is a country of forty million aristocrats, individualists all! That, do not forget, may be why we are so hard to govern!

And what an aristocrat, in all those senses, was Anatole France! No one—and that is one of the traits of his manner and his genius—ever carried to greater perfection that subtle gentleness, that grace in the expression of all things, even violent, subversive or merely unconventional things, which is the equivalent in literature of good manners among the great. Such qualities, be it noted, do not fail to dissemble a certain haughtiness, nor a sense of superiority not to be discussed. But Anatole France, nevertheless, remained the "petty-bourgeois" Parisian, by virtue of his love of politics, and of that urban, strictly urban, life, which underlies all French "urbanity," even in the less wealthy classes of our towns. All his life long, this son of a retail bookseller continued to love, and associate with, his own humble kind. Only with them, I believe, did he feel altogether at ease. And how well he knew them! To such happy understanding we owe the little gem called *Crainquebille*, in which the policeman, a lowly representative of the law, speaks as pointedly and with as great richness of philosophy, as the poor devil whom he is taking to court, speaks of his miseries! There is no slang in these immortal pages, a strange gentility, rather; and—another trait of France's admirable style—usage of the most ordinary adjectives, which are thrown into interesting relief by the places in which he manages to drop them: "numerous, smooth, full days," says Crainquebille!

Crainquebille is a story only a few pages long. As I said earlier, France was first of all and above all a short story writer: the truly finished portions of his work are short stories. He liked the literary "gem," the perfect jewel in a perfect setting, the "page" fit to go into a textbook—things on the style of Montesquieu's *Dialogue of Sulla and Eucrates.* It is a striking fact that his novels, the long ones, his admirable *Gods Athirst* and *Thaïs*, were first written as short stories (for a newspaper, the *Journal des Débats*) and lengthened afterwards by dialogues and digressions (not by new episodes).

There can be no complaint at this. These digressions, these dialogues, are sometimes sumptuous and always admirable. Where can one find more dispassionate views on Napoleon than those inserted in *The Red*

Lily? Where better "talk" than the remarks of the Abbé Lantaigne, of Masure, of Bergeret, in *l'Orme du Mail?* Where better essays on the conflict of faiths and dogmas than those woven into the adventures of Thaïs and Paphnuce? Neither their charm, nor their lightness of touch, nor their scepticism, can prevent perception of their depth and their tendency. It is a Voltaire revised by a Renan, but remaining much more Voltaire than Renan. No mercy, and, if not a formal condemnation, at least a sort of mistrustful disdain, toward everything not deriving from the philosophical traditions of Antiquity and of the Eighteenth century!

There were two causes for this turn of mind in Anatole France. That was the turn of mind of the petty-bourgeoisie of the Second Empire of which France, paradoxically, became the interpreter. Hugo has been mischievously styled "an epic National Guardsman." France was not a guardsman, nor was he "epic." He did not like Hugo. And he did not like—in this with better reason—Béranger. I heard him chant one day:

> *Quel démon tremble et s'agite*
> *Sur ce grabat, qu'il fleurit?*
> *C'est l'amour, qui rend visite*
> *À la pauvreté qui rit.*

"Charming!" he commented. "Unfortunately, that's all there is!"

And yet, there was a good deal of Béranger in Anatole France—he was a Béranger with genius. The idea offered to mankind by Christianity, and especially by the Catholic Church, was the reverse of his own. The Church's methods of action and surveillance, its enduring patience in aiming at temporal control over societies, filled him with dread. Paradoxically again, he retained, deep down in him, something of the Republicans of 1848. Ridiculous dreamers, thinking vulgarly and stupidly of great things! But those great things were the things Voltaire, the Encyclopedists, the Eighteenth century, had aspired to! So if we imagine this great spirit, this magnificent, ironical and violent writer (under his perpetual softness and politeness of expression, he was as violent as Racine, his God)—if we imagine him as attempting to straddle the political and moral ideas of the French *bourgeoisie* of the Second Empire and the ideas of the Eighteenth century which provoked them, we shall have a very fair impression of his mind.

France, however, transformed the ideas in question, lifting them to the heights of his own genius, by going back, on the one hand, to the purest fountainhead of Hellenism, and on the other—a thing that would have astonished him, had any one ever called it to his attention—by cherishing at the same time a deep faith in one of the basic dogmas of Christianity—the doctrine of original sin. France thought of men as evil, bloodthirsty animals—there was no Rousseau in him. But men were not animals like other animals: before their weak and unsteady eyes, as they groped their way forward through the dark and through crime, there flickered an eternal, unextinguishable light: the idea of Justice. Our worship, therefore, to Themis, mother of the gods and of men! And—it follows, since France did not believe in any future life, but only in this one —let this poor miserable existence on earth be made as endurable as possible! We must hate murder! We must hate jealousy, the cause of murder! We must hate that collective murder known as war, and militarism, therefore, at once cause and result of war!

It is, accordingly, easy to understand France's attitude in the Dreyfus case, which split our country into two camps: in the one, as he saw it, Themis, an unfortunate (a reminiscence of Voltaire as defender of Calas); in the other, the military clique, and the Clerical clique, allied in the service of a criminal and beastly error. But the same premises do not account for his embracing Socialism. I have good grounds for believing that if he loved what the people of his generation called "the Republic," he was not fond of republicans and especially not of republican politicians.

He thought them a vulgar, petty, intriguing crowd, always surrendering to "realise" unworthy aims. But there was also his love of mischief, his yearning for freedom. These inclined him to stand with an Opposition. And which Opposition? That of the extreme Right? But it was peopled by men whom he scorned and ridiculed—Churchmen, generals! Such an affiliation would deprive him of the privilege of saying anything on any subject! "Just consider the case of poor Jules Lemaître," he used to say. "Since he has been with them, he hasn't opened his mouth! . . . No,—you see, it's this way: when a man has attained a certain reputation in letters, he must be clever enough to choose a lost cause." By which he meant that he could enroll only in a party which, in his lifetime at least, promised never to rise to Power. Socialism seemed to fit his case. He was greatly embarrassed when the Russian Revolution suddenly made Communism a government. But he pronounced his blessing in ringing words which certain acts of his belied. Already an aged man, he doubtless reflected: "The *status quo* will probably last as long as I do!"

He died in a glory richly deserved. No reputation since Hugo's had been so universally recognized. But hardly had the torches of his State funeral been snuffed, than a reaction set in. There were those who found the author of *Orme du Mail* just a witty columnist, writing from hand to mouth in virtue of an "intellectual anarchism."

Just what such critics could have been working from is not very clear to me. What is as clear as day is that, under an affectedly ironical surface, France propounded a noble and rich philosophy, the philosophy which has determined the present-day aspects of civilization in the West. If I have tried to lay bare the motives of some of his attitudes, it has been because I well remember one of his remarks which contained a lesson of great significance to me. He was at work on *Gods Athirst* one day, when he exclaimed: "It's not getting on—I am stopped!" I smiled. Anatole France "stopped" by a literary problem! The idea seemed ridiculous to me. "Yes," he resumed, "I'm stopped! My man, Gamelin, is turning out a hero!" "Well?" "Well! I must be off the track!"

By which he meant that, most often, our more extraordinary and heroic deeds find their origin in very matter-of-fact motives—a truth, alas, which our writers have only too well grasped. Heroism is as absent from the novels of France as they are from those of the Goncourts! But I too have been looking for certain factors in France's talent in little out-of-the-way things. I have not succeeded so well, for his talent was vast. He was high enough above the rest of men to see them clearly. That is why the Abbé Lantaigne, Mazure, Bergeret, the delightful Jérôme Coignard, without being "types" of Balzacian or Stendhalian stature, exist and are not forgotten. Then, his hedonism, his philosophy which taught that life is to be enjoyed, lent his work not only grace and charm, but gaiety as well. Coignard and his adventures are gay, frankly so. In whom, indeed, shall we soon be finding such a precious gift for gaiety? Finally there is his style, his enchanting style. Critics have tried to detect in it the double influence of the petticoaters of the Seventeenth century and of Renan. I cannot see that. France's French is a French of the late Nineteenth century, sublimated, felt, through a mastering of all our great writers over four centuries past— or better, three centuries past. The Nineteenth century is not at all in evidence. If we are to call it anything, why not call it plain "Anatole France"—the style of a supreme, original, inimitable artist?

XIV

PAUL BOURGET

I STILL recall the profound emotion which the generation that was young toward the end of the last century experienced on reading *Le Disciple*. *Crime d'Amour, Cruelle Énigme, Mensonges*, had been novels that made them look upon Bourget as a society psychologist, more adroit than original. *André Cornélis* had seemed to them only an ingenious, though somewhat clumsy, attempt to revive psychology through a form of detective story. But in *Le Disciple* those young people recognized themselves.

To be sure they discerned the artificiality in the work, its eclecticism in inspiration and in literary methods. If Stendhal had not created Julien Sorel, would there ever have been a Robert Greslou, a man who came from nothing, a scholarship-student at the University, just as Sorel had been in a seminary, and, like Sorel, making his way as tutor into an aristocratic family, and seducing the daughter through sheer will and self-assertion, as Sorel seduced Mme. de Rênal? And just as *The Red and the Black* had been suggested to Stendhal by a criminal trial in the Jura, did not *The Chambiges Case* inspire *Le Disciple*? It was a time when Positivist materialism had not only revived the historic

method of Taine, but also the psycho-physiology of
Ribot. The Chambiges in question was a man probably
not without talent. He was at work on a book which
would have been called *La Dispersion infinitésimale
du Moi* ("The Infinitesimal Dispersion of the Ego")
—almost a Barrès title, even at that early date! In the
course of a journey to Algeria he had lured a virtuous
Protestant girl from the straight and narrow path. Unable to live with each other, also unable to endure
separation, the two lovers went to a deserted villa, after
a supreme love-feast, to commit suicide, singing in the
carriage as they drove alone: "Hail, last dawn of mine!"
The poor woman died instantly. Chambiges, danger-
ously hurt, was unlucky enough to survive. I met the
unhappy wretch later on, in 1897, as a volunteer in the
Greek army where he had signed up to fight the Turks:
to such an extent were Byronic and Romantic memories still vivid in the minds of those self-styled ego-
tists! Still later he published, under the pseudonym of
Lamy, a novel or two that had no success.

At that date, there were still a few great Romanticists left. I do not speak of them here at length because their works are but the fruits—albeit savory ones
—of a powerful school in its late autumn. Certain of
those last Romanticists, such as Villiers de l'Isle-Adam,
author of the marvelously beautiful *Contes Cruels* and

the mystical and musical *Axel*, were steeped in Wagnerian æsthetics. And gorgeous Barbey d'Aurevilly—who had awarded himself a title, just as Balzac did—was combining a brilliant, oratorical style, and a fertile imagination, with a sense of the heroic, the chivalrous, the "Musketeerish," and an inclination for the exaggerated, the fantastic, and even the impossible. Imagine! In his *Chevalier Destouches*, certain "gentlemen," making a crossing from England to France in the course of the fights in the Vendée, throw their oars overboard to lighten their boats, and row with their guns! For all such things, in *Vielle Maîtresse*, in *Le Prêtre Marié*, in *L'Ensorcelé* and in *Les Diaboliques*, there are superb pages, and not a little dramatic suspense arising from well-devised plots.

But both Villiers and Barbey came together on one point: a reversion, literary at least, to Catholicism and horror for the democracy and materialism then prevailing. And, in adition to Taine, Stendhal, and memories (still fresh) of the Chambiges suicide-pact, it was the influence of Barbey that Bourget felt most strongly.

But, however that may be, the same psychological crisis which drove Greslou to a quasi-assassination, to the Criminal Courts, to the point of "drama," was working in all the young men of the time. And they felt the presence of the crisis in *Le Disciple*. Following individual tendencies or preferences, they booed or applauded; but in any event they were stirred, one and all, to the depths of their souls. This novel furthermore revealed Bourget to himself. At least for his readers, Bourget's development dates from *Le Disciple*. At that moment his spiritual evolution was about complete. It led him to the same views to which, later on, Maurras will come.

Supposing we state them!

Bourget adopts the conclusions of Taine, which are on the whole, those of Auguste Comte: the Revolution of 1789 was—a mess! Men are not equal! It is dangerous to give them direct access to the high offices in the State, to let them climb all the rungs of the social ladder in one lifetime. If men are to keep their morality and their self-respect, they must climb slowly through the efforts of several successive generations, supported by strict religious discipline—a matter perhaps of centuries! A man—or a woman—starting from the bottom of the ladder, may themselves exemplify desirable virtues. Not so their children: the ascent has been too sudden for them; they are left dizzy, they fly wild! The slow, graduated degrees which the Old Régime ordained for such climbs are indispensable. (In this regard *Le Disciple* preludes *l'Étape*, a book written many years later, and Bourget's final culminating effort.)

Now all this is a thesis. From a literary point of view we need not ask whether it be false or true. But it raises the question of the literary value of the "thesis-novel." The latter is not provoked directly by observation of people. It subordinates character and plot to the demonstration of the thesis. The process reminds one of the old comic recipe for making a canon: "First take a hole and pour molten brass around it." The thesis-novel takes a hole and improves on it. To succeed in such a *genre*, to give a novel conceived in this manner some appearance of reality, requires a great talent indeed. Unquestionably Paul Bourget had the talent: a talent made up of a high-grade intelligence and in which the intelligence drives itself to a somewhat arbitrary, artificial, portrayal of life. We must remember that following on a few experiments in poetry (verse makes an excellent apprenticeship for a prose writer since it teaches him to balance his sentence and pack it with matter) Bourget was first of all a critic. His *Essais de Psychologie Contemporaine*, which he fumigated later on to delete all opinions that he judged no longer orthodox, remains one of his best works. If thereafter he turned to the novel, it was because, as he says himself, the "novel is the most modern of all literary forms and the one most easily adaptable to the varying needs of each human nature."

The novel form was a choice of his intelligence, not of his temperament.

And there is another difficulty: the reader is a little wary of the thesis-novel. We say to ourselves: "If the author shows us his characters acting the way they do, performing such and such acts, it is because he wants them to act like that. But would they act that way in reality? Does a university education necessarily throw a boy born of the masses into amorality? Do all the descendants of aristocrats and people of wealth— give them as much 'family' as may seem required— become incapable of certain compromises?"

This criticism bears least seriously on the *Démon du Midi*, which is a fine psychological drama. Further-more it is to be noted that Bourget's Catholic and neo-monarchical attitude, which became more positive as the years went by and cost him a certain unpopularity with the generations preceding the War, has won him the esteem, admiration and respect of the generations following the War. A certain number of our young men today incline either to a return to Catholicism (with a dash of heresy) or toward dissatisfaction with the democratic system. And sometimes toward both!

XV

MAURICE BARRÈS

THAT predominance of intelligence over imagination, which amounts at times to imaginative barrenness, is a trait more conspicuous in Barrès than in Bourget. In Barrès you will also find the thesis novel and the same hostility toward parliamentary democracy; but with a more detached (though respectful) attitude towards Catholicism (for Barrès too is a traditionalist). Furthermore there is the same tendency toward an eclectic style in which one feels the influence of Renan, of Chateaubriand, and even of Stendhal—but with the addition of something that is peculiarly of Barrès.

At the same time this determined adversary of parliamentary democracy has a taste for politics, as Anatole France had, but in a different, more active way. Barrès will go to Parliament himself. He will think he owes it to "the doctrine," to the "myth," of which he has been the eloquent prophet and the literary creator—Nationalism, to become a deputy and express himself in action. This great, this admirable rhetorician worships energy and heroism, as Stendhal did; and he is eager to play a rôle, a public rôle, a great rôle, as Disraeli did (he studied Disraeli carefully). The rôle he actually plays will be more of surfaces and appearances than of depth; for no one was ever more strictly a "man of letters" than Barrès. To point the contrast, just consider "little old man Combes" whom he despised and defamed but who—nobody that he was, a nobody who knew provincial France through and through!—managed to hold his place at the head of the government for more than three years, to expel the Congregations from France and pave the way for the separation of Church and State! Barrès, in a word, is d'Annunzio rather than Mussolini.

This is the impression one gets of Barrès at a hasty glance. But there is something else—a something whereby he is both original and influential. The power he was never able to wield in active politics he exercised as a master upon the generation which has been reading his books; and he will continue to exercise it in the future. The fact is, he is a real discoverer, a real innovator. Very Romantic at heart, as witness his fondness for Chateaubriand, another sublime rhetorician, he goes beyond the Romanticists in that he synthesizes feeling and intelligence: I do not mean that there was no intelligence in the feeling of the Romanticists, but they did not strive for it; and when they chanced to be intelligent, they tried to pretend that they had not done so on purpose! With Barrès it is quite the contrary!

Thinking, as much thinking as possible, that there may be as much feeling as possible when thought has been fired and made will in emotion—such was Barrès's bold effort to reconcile Romanticism, which finds its roots in sentiment, with Classicism, which stresses intelligence (to such a degree that the literary vehicle devised to express the violent passions of a passionate man like Racine will seem the quintessence of the rational). It matters little that Barrès does not always succeed, that often the "thought" which he emotionalizes is not so much "thought" as a formula which he has passionately embraced, and which becomes in consequence mere "development," mere asseveration. This is an almost unavoidable defect in the method. But when Barrès succeeds, he finds intonations of gripping intensity. This is the case with his landscapes, landscapes conceived and expressed as true "pathos" in the etymological sense of the term, as true "experience," his "ego" permeating its object, transforming it, absorbing it.

"The cult of the ego" is chapter one of the Barrès gospel. Since he was not above startling and even shocking people who take words in their ordinary meanings (the holy horror of such people makes fine

publicity), he hammered insistently on his "egoïsm."
Really it meant nothing more terrible than that the
duty of every man, and especially of every artist, requires him to "find himself," and to assimilate all
he can of the Universe about him. *L'Homme Libre,
Sous l'oeil des Berbères, L'Ennemi des Lois* are, if
one consider them carefully, nothing but manuals of a
spiritual (and passionate) gymnastic—a scheme of
training for the discovery of oneself in the Universe.
In the same way the *Imitation* tries to be a manual
of spiritual exercises for the soul which would seek
God in itself (with a similar stirring of passions). It
is a pity that Barrès never took time to develop this
evident paradox. His genius would surely have developed from that process some of those startling effects of which he was otherwise so fond.

But the effort to bring one's ego to a conquest of the
Universe is to recreate the Universe, glorify it, char-
acterise it, in one's own terms, just as Napoleon does.
The Universe, notice, not just some part of the Universe! Perhaps Barrès was not far from doing so! Did
he not write, in one of those calculated confessions in
which he mingled the disillusioned haughtiness of a
Chateaubriand with an irony altogether his own: "Had
I thought of the world the way I have thought of Lorraine, I would be in truth a citizen of humanity"?

However, as everybody knows, he did not go quite that far. In making this ingenious effort to apprehend his ego, he encounters, as properly and necessarily he had to encounter, a collectivity just beyond his ego. And he stopped at Lorraine, then later at the nation of which Lorraine forms a part. . . . This may perhaps have been because the great Romanticists, Hugo, Michelet, Quinet (Quinet is unreadable today, though he exerted quite an influence on young men of the past), had used the humanity theme. But it is especially because Frenchmen like Barrès and all Frenchmen who read books, are much more conscious, first of their little neighborhood and next of France, than they are of a still vague, still eminently theoretical "humanity." Humanity is still an intellectual concept, while our notions of "home" and "homeland" are surcharged with sentiments and memories of our own lives and those of our fathers. We might imagine "humanity" developing some such richness of emotional connotation; but we should have to suppose some extraordinary or fantastic experience, such as an invasion of the Earth by dangerous, non-human beings— the Martians of Wells or the Xipehus of Rosny. And yet it is amusing to note—in spite of Well's pretensions to Socialism he is so much of a Britisher that his Martian invasion takes place, in the face of all plausibilities, on his little English island only—and he manifests no interest at all in the attitude of humanity at large toward a menace that would be unquestionably universal. . . .

Bear in mind, on the other hand, that there is only one religion which still in our time can ask of the majority of men, nay, of the almost unanimity of men, unreserved devotion, utter abnegation, the very sacrifice of their lives. We must even go farther: there is only one religion which, barring exceptions, still makes martyrs and regards martyrdom as a natural and necessary thing. I refer to patriotism—and patriotism is the same thing as Nationalism (dropping from the acceptation of this latter word such connotations of reaction as French publicists have crowded into it). The evidence is before our eyes: the late War, in four years' time, made fifteen millions of martyrs in Europe and in America; and they are virtually the only martyrs in our day who are honored with monuments and ossaria! The homeland! The land where we were born and where our ancestors were born—our mother who gave us birth, and our father who gave us sustenance and admonished us: "These are the rules of life!"— rules of that Church within whose walls every child has believed in a particular God and said his prayers! Such things are part of our very flesh! Such things make up our "selves"! When Barrès protested that he had written only a single book in the whole course of his literary (and political) life—*l'Homme libre* (manual of egotism that it is) and that his Nationalism came from his egoism the way fruit comes from a tree, he was not exaggerating. Furthermore his sentimental "elaborations," expressed in an acidly original manner, supplied a necessary dignity as "thought" to ill-defined but singularly powerful sentiments in the young men who were reading him or were about to do so.

And here again was style, a magic of style! This great sorcerer of Art—a great Romanticist at bottom—rejuvenated the Romantic faith by giving it a new language adapted to such intellectualization of sentiment. It was the rôle of Barrès to bestow on "the words of the tribe" if not purer, at least more youthful, meanings; and so true is this that even today, thirty years later, certain writers such as Drieu de la Rochelle (one of the most intelligent) still recognize what they owe to him; and, while repudiating almost all of Barrès's doctrine of ideas, keep, along with contrary and adverse theories, much of his vocabulary, rhythm, and method of composition. We still have a Barrès style, though we do not have and have never had (in any writer of importance) an imitation of Anatole France (inimitable indeed!). Writers like M. Joseph Delteil

who refuse to "write Barrès" and studiously avoid his
manner, manifestly do so by way of reaction, and otherwise express for his writing not so much respect as
youthful, enthusiastic, admiration. Delteil regretted
that Barrès should have "missed Napoleon"! How
warmly, indeed, he would have felt the Corsican! What
a drawing of him he would have given us, what a
vigorous, colorful, tigerish picture!

I referred above to the formulas, the "ideologies"
which Barrès embroidered with passion. That was what
Barrès did most and best. Even his novels are "ideologies"; "Uprooted" (*Déracinés*) for example, which is
an effort to translate into life (*i.e.* into the semblance
of life) his thesis of the "little homeland," the roots
of which one must nurture ever, not in one's heart
only, but in one's thought. And yet this counterfeit
Lorrainian, born in Auvergne, as dark-haired and olive-
skinned as Spaniard ever was, is too intelligent not to
betray that his Sturel, like himself, attains originality
only by pulling himself up by the roots. And there are
nationalistic "ideologies" too! The three novels on
énergie nationale! Life, real life, action, appears in
them for the most part only as stucco! But what stucco!
How deeply some of these pages moved the young
men of the time! What new dreams they awakened
about Alsace and Lorraine, which had hitherto been

accorded hardly more than a platonic remembrance. Women said: "I cannot read *Colette Baudoche* without trembling all over." And I could mention the case of a French statesman, a Deputy in Parliament who confessed to me some twenty years ago—he was quite young at the time—that *Déracinés* had not a little colored his personal ambitions and his conceptions of political life (his name was André Tardieu)! But it was all "ideology" at best, with almost no imagination. That is why Barrès had to be ever refreshing his thought in new landscapes: *Un Amateur d'Âmes, Du Sang, de la Volupté, de la Mort,* even the *Jardin de Bérénice,* the *Voyage de Sparte,* the *Greco. La Colline inspirée* is a noble piece of work, one of his noblest— but it is not a novel! For the lack of imagination, the general incompetence in plot-making, the insufficient "plausibility," to be noted today in our most recent French fiction, Barrès may be partly responsible. He pushed his successors in the direction of their bent.

Barrès marks the culminating point of Nationalism regarded as the principal factor in literary emotion. One may imagine a mountain chain rising on one side in gentle hills and pretty valleys, on the other in a bluff escarpment. Barrès stands on the brink of the latter. In the abyss below him—fifteen millions of martyrs to his religion, in four years! One stands

aghast! One hesitates! That is too many! One might be
tempted to prefer the broad humanism, nay, the anti-
militarism of an Anatole France, and to prophesy for
these a more abiding literary survival!

Though, to be sure, the facts seem to be against us!
After the atrocious struggle of the recent past, the
great European Powers may be feeling the limitations
of their nationalistic ideals. But there are others among
the younger ones—Czecho-Slovakia, Yugoslavia, Poland, Italy, and even Russia, who continue, as is only
too apparent at this moment, to feel the need of having
those ideals stated, stressed, and featured, for them,
in terms overheated with emotion. Then, and especially,
there are the nations and races of the distant East—
Egypt, Arabia, Syria, the vast world of China, India,
Indo-China—which are just awakening to the concept
of national and social unity. I can imagine Barrès being
translated fifty years from now, and perhaps sooner,
into strange languages that have no connection with
the Western tongues, and unchaining enthusiasms and
passions which have long since been extinguished in
our part of the world. Is not that already the case with
Voltaire and Rousseau, who are now driving those
distant peoples to intoxication while we have anti-
dotized and digested what certain people still call their
"poison"? Suppose Barrès should have the same luck,

as the author of the trilogy on *énergie nationale*! I imagine that his ghost, still haughtily inclined, would acknowledge the honor and contemplate results with a smile of injured innocence. Just another of those dramas of the struggle between life and death which so fascinated him!

XVI

ROMAIN ROLLAND

NEVERTHELESS, the spread of Barrès's thought abroad, and especially to what might be called the "far abroad," may meet one obstacle: the very artistry of his expression. The case of artistic prose is that of great, truly great, poetry: its verbal enchantment gone, little may be left of it in translation.

Romain Rolland escapes this menace. He could be called "European" even before the War, more European than French. He was being read in translation in many languages, and particularly in German. He has, however, a similarity, at least an external one, with Barrès: he too is not only, nor even especially, a novelist, but a creator of formulæ, of "ideologies." Barrès goes looking for lessons in passion to El Greco, and at Toledo. Rolland looks for lessons in the heroic to Michelangelo and Beethoven; and—a curious thing!—his heroic, even in his *Michel Angelo,* has something Wagnerian about it. This tall, angular, rather lean individual (he was lean, at any rate, as a young man) is a music lover and a fanatical and idealizing lover of Wagner. Some thirty years ago he said to me: "I prefer reading music to studying it out at the piano. I follow the movement better, the decorative line."

It was through music, especially through the greatest, richest, most inspiring, and (in Wagner) most heroic, German music, that he made his first contacts and finally his friendship with Germany. It was also through music that, quite understandably, he became as devotedly an Internationalist as Barrès was a Nationalist, and almost at the same moment—just a few years later. Music, in fact, is a universal language. There is no art more exquisitely international.

In those days, nobody in France (save a few University students, who were to prove extremely useful during the War) knew anything about Germany. That country was viewed from afar with mingled sentiments of bitterness, mistrust and fear. No one wanted a war to get back Alsace and Lorraine—not even, really, our Nationalists of the Barrès type; they exploited French sympathies and regrets for the lost provinces more as a "myth" to focus patriotic emotions. Germany was thought of as a possible enemy, whose industrial and military power was growing day by day, and every day becoming more dangerous; and the Germans were a brutal vulgar race, without charm, without civilization. And lo, Rolland suddenly transported us into the heart of a Germany surviving in the little towns along the Rhine, a land of simple, naïf, patriarchal manners and customs, with a culture made up more of heart than of mind, and revealing itself in music! Good souls, splendid people, indifferent to "Vaterland," or at least to the materialistic, political conception of the "Vaterland" as "will to power"! And this, because they were music-lovers and therefore internationalists, holding that any country where there was music was home to them! Europeans, by the grace and favor of music!

The sensation, in France, was profound! The first volumes of *Jean Christophe*, issued in the pretty "Fortnightly Miscellany" (*Cahiers de la Quinzaine*) of Péguy, so hard to find today, were literally devoured. The Dreyfus business had just shaken things up, opening the minds of a portion of our public to ideas of a different order; while others, hurt, humiliated, beaten, were turning for consolation to Barrès. But there is a trait about the French mind that does honor to its sense of fairness. Since the Nationalists were having their say, the country felt an instinctive compulsion to listen to the contrary thesis, have a look at the other side of such an important question. This independence, I may add, this individualism, explains why we find it much harder than is the case in Germany, England, or the United States, to create public opinion overnight. France "thinks as one man" only in the face of some great emergency such as war, or under pressure of strenuous censorship.

And in Germany, the delight was greater still! People were enchanted! "At last a Frenchman who does not insult us, who even seems to like us!" "Neutral" Switzerland, divided among three nationalities, was the first to see the advantages of a friendly understanding among the peoples of Europe. And the Protestant countries followed suit. As a result of Tolstoy's deep influence upon him, Rolland, a Catholic, born of an actively Catholic mother, "thought Protestant," as it were in spite of himself. At times, indeed, he is half an evangelist!

The huge success of *Jean Christophe*, on the Continent and beyond, was also furthered to some extent by the fact that the novel was not "good writing." Not that Rolland had not passed his courses in composition at the *École normale*! Especially in the final revision of his *Beethoven*, there are some magnificent and very eloquent pages, pages, as I believe, more richly significant than many of the half-factitious, somewhat overstrained, portions of Barrès's *Greco*. Rolland, indeed, can at times try too hard to "write well" —he studied too hard in school, and remembered too much. I am thinking of the counterfeit Rabelaisianisms in his *Colas Breugnon*. But he is not worrying about style in his *Jean Christophe*! It is the sentence and vocabulary of everybody, with not a little carelessness, not a few commonplaces, and, as for length of wind . . . ! But the point is: a style of that kind goes very well in translation! Furthermore, most Germans, not to say, most Anglo-Saxons, are less fussy about such things than we French.

Finally, in *Aube*, in *Adolescence*, in fact, all through the first two or three volumes of that endless, over-stuffed, badly managed *Jean Christophe*, one stumbles on paragraphs of surpassing freshness, simplicity and naturalness, this last a quality so often lacking in our literature; and also on an echo, faint, to be sure, but none the less engaging, of the sort of sensitiveness Rousseau displays in the first sections of the *Confessions*. Unforgettable some of these turns of expression, so apt, so fraught with a heavy, slow-moving, very Germanic gaiety and good-nature! The remark of Jean Christophe's uncle, an expressman, as the boy sits at the piano trying his first "compositions": "Why do you do that, sonny? Nobody asked you to!" Words I somehow always remember, and which fit so many situations, especially many of the books that are being written these days! And the uncle registers again, if you remember—there where, in Lamartine fashion, he stands on a hilltop looking down into a romantic valley and singing in perfect voice two of the finest folk-songs of old Germany. "One more, uncle!" cries Jean Christophe, enraptured. "Never more than two, sonny!" Most salutary insight! The emotions become frothy if art and the artist dwell upon them too long!

An insight, alas, that Rolland did not always have available in *Jean Christophe*! Even his most fanatical admirers were overtaxed by the unendurably tiresome *Foire sur la Place*—a mere piece of pamphleteering; and, in *The Burning Bush* all that portion devoted to describing a labor riot is out of place and a plain nuisance; for *The Burning Bush* is a book of magnificent inspiration, expressing all the fire and intelligent passionateness of a born music-lover. The theme is Wagner's infatuation with Madame Wensendouk, which had been utilized already by another novelist, Édouard Rod, in *A Shadow Falls on the Mountain.* Rod was a competent man of letters, conscientious, careful. Read his book, and then Rolland's! You will get some idea of their differing talents!

Yet even *La Foire sur la Place*, useless and annoying as it is, has some amazing phrases that strike one by their exactness and their comprehensive concentration. "The Frenchman is pessimistic about other people, optimistic about himself." Translate: "People are lunatics, one and all! But I know what I am about!" An epitome on the extreme individualism of the French! And there is something to it. The Frenchman, as a rule, does make a good try, as an individual.

There is a danger that *Jean Christophe*, in spite of the very great beauties of *Michael Angelo* and *Beethoven*, may be generally accepted as Rolland's masterpiece. In spite of its faults, its platitudes, it is a stirring thing—it lives. Not *Clérambault*, not *Colas Breugnon*, will ever dethrone it, even if the famous *Above the Mêlée*, which Rolland published in Switzerland just after the outbreak of the War, had never been written. To reread this book now, when atmospheres have changed, is to feel that Rolland may not have been altogether wrong in trying to remain "European" during that terrible conflict. But he was wrong, nevertheless! In case of war a man has to "play with his team," stand with his country, whatever the cost to his conscience. That is one of the canons of the sportsman's code. But Rolland was not a sportsman. He was a pure intellectual, as intellectuals were in those days—as Barrès, for that matter, was, as Jules Lemaître was, and so many others! . . .

I remember I once had the honor of being invited to Lemaître's house on the occasion of my having written something or other for which he chose to congratulate me. I was a boy twenty years old at the time.

It was not a long business on his part, in fact, not longer than the thing deserved; and then he veered to Barrès and, as was only proper, went into greater detail. But I interrupted him: "I do not share your admiration!" (I have changed my mind since.) "I have just read a certain *Amateur d'Âmes*. Though my copy bears a dedication in his hand that is most flattering to me, I find it utter trash!"

"Trash! How's that?" Lemaître was properly shocked, but he was interested.

"Well," I resumed, with the fierce and unfair impetuousness of youth. "You see, I'm a swimmer. . . . In a description of Toledo, early in the book, he talks about a man swimming upstream in the river just below the town. A man doesn't swim that way, especially against the current! Barrès never swam! He doesn't know how it is done. Why does he talk about things he doesn't understand? . . . Just mush!"

Lemaître spread his two hands—he was too polite to shrug his shoulders—as though to say: "What on earth does that matter?"

And yet, there are people today, Montherlant, for example (he knows his Barrès), who would understand me perfectly . . . !

XVII

THE LADIES

THERE had been George Sand's: *Indiana*: woman's right to emancipation, her right to love—and "Love as God," to whom it was a "religious" duty not to resist! To read this book today is almost as much of a task as to read the *Nouvelle Héloïse*, its source and precursor. In the history of literature, however, and in the history of manners, it holds, as the *Nouvelle Héloïse* holds, an importance that must not be disregarded. Assuredly it is not through *Indiana* that George Sand will continue to make posthumous conquests of hearts, the only conquests her ardent soul, so "good," so "strong," and so "innocent" at the same time, can hope to make in the Elysian Fields. It is rather through *La petite Fadette, François le Champi,* and *La Mare au Diable* (especially), "peasant" tales packed with false sentimentality but also with eternally charming impressions of Nature. Proust avowed his gratitude to her for just those things; for Proust had the very rare gift of retaining fresh and unspoiled the memories of the first literary joys of his boyhood.

But *Indiana* is still the most important by far. Had it not been for *Indiana* and others of Sand's books, which keep to the same theme with equal conviction, along with a "poetry" so rich as to border on vulgarity, there might well have been no *Madame Bovary*! Emma Bovary is an Indiana of the French *bourgeoisie*, made a little ridiculous at first, in Flaubert's intention, which gradually changed as the book advanced and he conceived a greater and greater pity for her—the case of Cervantes and Don Quixote over again. Yet Flaubert had seen clearly. In the women of his time, and even later, great reserve was apparent, restraint, shyness, and remorse, on occasion—at least it was good form for women to feel such things—along with rash and reckless impulses; and they appear in Madame Rênal of *Le Rouge et le Noir*, and all the way along to the mad and unhappy Emma Bovary.

The fact doubtless is that till a fairly late date under the Third Republic women received no other education than that of the convent schools, which kept them as far as possible in ignorance of sex. In the East this ignorance was never cultivated. A substitute for it was found in cloistering under eunuch guardianship. Moral cloistering through ignorance, the idea of sin as a sort of spiritual eunuch—such the formidably ingenious device of the West!

Nevertheless, the girls and women of the West, the French women of those days, had their sex and were conscious of it, to greater or lesser degrees of vividness. More sentimental than men by nature, they tended to subordinate desire to sentiment, failing which they could only (without much effort) express desire as sentiment.

All this has changed in the course of the last thirty years. Female education has drawn closer and closer to the training given young men. Whereas in eras past there were books forbidden to women down to their wedding day, and, for such as heeded the counsel of their spiritual advisors and confessors, down to the day of their death, now our girls and women can read, and do read, everything the boys and the men read; and they are just as "well-informed" as men about things they formerly did not know or were supposed not to know.

Birth control, furthermore, has spread. It began appearing in France, among the aristocratic and society classes, early in the Eighteenth century. In course of time it made its way through all strata of our population, reaching the rural masses, curiously enough, with the help of the State itself! The learned researches of the statistician Levasseur have shown how, early in the Nineteenth century, some alarm was felt lest increasing population in France exceed the resources of the country and lead to pauperism. Big industry was at the time hardly on the horizon. No one dreamed it would ever need so many "hands," at the lowest possible wages! So the Prefects of His Majesty Louis the Eighteenth urged the French peasantry in some regions to have fewer children. It is a safe inference that practical methods were suggested along with the recommendation.

There was no open discussion of such practices for a long time. Fifty years ago our *bourgeois* families made timid allusion, sometimes, to "moral restrictions"—as though any moral and therefore "abstentionist" curb could avail against what François de Nantes, of Convention fame, described in the chaste jargon of his time as "the most obstreperous of the instincts." Today, birth control is a subject of current conversation. It has become a sort of dogma that is discussed in the presence of children and perhaps for their edification. The immoral thing is to have too many children! Salomon Reinach wrote his *Grec sans larmes* for the use of young girls. One could easily find a publisher for a pamphlet entitled: "Love without Danger" if such a treatise were necessary! There is still the question of "virginity," to which certain rapidly decreasing numbers in our population continue to attach some importance; but the "Semi-Virgins" (*Demi-vierges*) of Marcel Prévost is already almost forty years old!

Prévost began his career in letters with an excellent,

a courageous, novel on the education supplied to young women in France in the schools of the Jesuits: the *Scorpion*, a well-written book of keen observation. Between the *Semi-Virgins* and the *Male Virgin* he has gone on writing well, cleverly combining plot-interest with observation of facts; for the social consequences of transformations in feminine morals fascinate him, and he uses his talents ingeniously. If a host of women readers remain loyal to him, that is because he knows what is in their heads and just what they want to hear. His trick is to moralise on immoral subjects in accord with "old-fashioned" moral principles. A sort of Devil's advocate, he is liberal but prudently so, and brave (brave he surely is!) with deftness. To appreciate his merits in this regard one has only to compare him with writers who have commercialized the same "unpleasant" materials—the author of *La Garçonne,* for example. Marcel Prévost is to be considered, in a certain sense, the precursor of the feminine novel written by women.

Reading everything that men read, our girls and women also read more than men, either because they have more time, or, because, on the contrary, they have gained access to professions formerly reserved for men, and quite properly claim a right to the same independence; or, finally, because their curiosity is greater.

I believe curiosity is in some ways greater in women than in men. How else explain the recent success of *Amour, terre inconnue*? I am sure nobody but a woman could read Kessel's *Belle du jour* all the way through to the end! Women are satisfied if you talk about them, though they do the talking much better themselves!

Observe in the first place that many of them, for example, Gérard d'Houville, or Lucie Delarue-Mardrus, began by poetry, and continue as poets—Anna de Noailles, with peerless talent. The reason must be that, with women, love is the great thing, and that love is in essence lyrical. It is even Romantic! In his remarkable *Avenir de l'Intelligence*, Charles Maurras cries: "Romanticism, that's the enemy!" He has a clear vision of the Romanticism of our poetesses. Indeed from that he draws the inference that Romanticism must be in its death agony, reasoning as follows: "Romanticism is an affair of subjective egoism, excluding intelligence. Women, therefore, being exclusively subjective—all sentiment with a modicum of thought—are grasping at Romanticism just when men are letting it go!" Perhaps! But since the novel is primarily concerned with passion, one may also argue from the same premises that women can be splendid novelists.

In the first place, every woman, from the time she begins braiding her hair, has a story to tell, her own story, or the story she wishes were hers. She is essentially a day-dreamer, and the dream is the mother of invention. Besides she has an eye for detail. The trouble may be that that story, her story, or the one she wishes were hers, is the only one she has to tell! . . .

I must give you a sample of a woman-novel, a good one by virtue of careful writing, fairly amusing ingenuity, a strictly decent plot, an attractive childishness, shall I say: *La Neuvaine de Colette.* A girl of humble circumstances says a *neuvaine* before a Saint, male or female, I forget which, in her chamber, asking for a husband. The prayers over, the husband fails to show up; so the girl throws the Saint out of the window! The Saint falls on the head of a handsome young man who chances to be passing, and lays him flat. The girl (or rather her mother) rushes to his aid, picks him up, cares for him, and, naturally, he falls in love. They marry and have a good honest family of children. This novel was published by the *Revue des Deux Mondes.* It went through two hundred editions. The author was a lady named Jeanne Schultz. Everything she wrote thereafter failed. That was the one story she had to tell, the dream of her girlhood!

I said that the theme was decent. That was because the book was written forty years ago. Things have changed in the meantime. Nowadays our austere censors find in the woman-novel a peculiarly feminine form of salaciousness. It is not in the words, it is in the things. I have remarked that female education tends to approximate the education of the males, and that the religious check is no longer operative on women, and notably on women who write. In the old days a man might expatiate on the desires and ecstasies of his flesh. A woman could not. Later on, women rebelled against that interdict; and since the expression of desire and voluptuousness on the part of a woman was a new thing, it seemed original to some and revolting to others. By now, everybody has grown accustomed to it. The only drawback about such frenzy, from the literary point of view, is its excess of poetizing about moments which, in the eyes of the stronger sex, do not always seem worth so much ink.

Stendhal's Sanseverina and his Madame Rênal are women supremely alive. So is Flaubert's Madame Bovary. So is the Marneffe of Balzac. Male novelists seem able to dig live women out of their brains, as well as live men. Women writers certainly add to their female characters traits which only a woman could think of; but they can do only women! Colette's *Chéri* is an insignificant mannikin, a doll—for that matter just what she wanted him to be! But what talent, and what a fine place that talent has managed to win for itself in the literature of our time! Colette has visited the most out-of-the-way places, and loved and drawn animals, dogs, cats, canaries, in ways no one had thought of doing before. From the music-halls in particular she has brought home sketches that are marvelously saddening, cruel, caressing, coaxing. Coaxing! Feminine coaxing! That is the trait which characterizes the mood of our female writers and gives tone to their work. That is the form sensuality takes when it becomes sentiment in women—something at once animal and very human. In *Vagabond*, in *Retraite sentimentale*, in *Vrilles de la Vigne*, you will find a style that is direct, personal, coaxing, ensnaring (always feline!) and of unparalleled skill.

That our women novelists are hardly ever able to "set" a male character, I have just observed; but there are exceptions, as in the *House of Sin* of Tinayre, a virile, a perfect achievement. And I dare say that as the intellectual experiences of our women come more and more to resemble and equal men's, such exceptions will prove more numerous. Lucie Delarue-Mardrus and Marion Gilbert have both a sort of instinctive vigor and realism, which may perhaps derive from their Norman origins. Madame de Noailles remains in prose what she is in verse, a charming poetess. It must also be remarked that *The Conquest of Jerusalem* of Myriam Harry is a book of exceptional distinction and exceptional worth. That a woman of German-Russian-Jewish ancestry, whose mother tongue was the Arabic of Palestine, should succeed in writing a French so pure, so picturesque, so "intelligent," is, incidentally, a noteworthy proof of the position France still holds, intellectually speaking, in the Near East.

But one thing more, before I leave our ladies. I find it rather interesting that there should be a visible effort in France today to revive the "Catholic" novel. All of them are by men—not one by a woman ——!

I explain this on the theory that our women are still in their period of rebellion, or at least of emancipation. When they have won their freedom, are they going to have a reaction analogous to the one taking place among our male "converts"? My thought is this: If, then, they still retain the frankness in writing which they have been acquiring in their days of rebellion, they may give us "Catholic" novels marked by new and unheard of vehemence!

XVIII

SOME OTHERS, OF THE SAME TIME

WHILE talking one day with Anatole France, I remember remarking that the Bergeret series would undoubtedly be the only picture left of the manners of our pre-war period. "You are mistaken," he replied, "there is Hermant!" And he drew for me such a vivid sketch of Abel Hermant's talent that I shall always remember it in its most subtle details.

There may have been some generosity on his part in this. Gossip has it that Mme. de Caillavet's salon, where France was enthroned like a god on Olympus, came in for some little ridicule at the hands of the author of *Les Renards*. But France harbored no rancor on that account. "A little inhuman," he said of Hermant. "But that's probably because he is still a good deal of a child. Children are tender and disarming, but they are selfish, though we must not hold that against them. They are gay, they are roguish by nature. The world, in their eyes, is a game. It is a game to Hermant. He does not take it altogether seriously; he is even grateful to it for being what it is. He would be utterly astonished should anyone take offense at some of the things he says. He scratches, he likes to cuff . . . but without venom. And what pictures he paints! See here now, since we have come to that—suppose we take our comparisons from painting! Hermant is not in the manner of the great Italians, or of the great Hollanders. He reminds you of our old French school from Bouilly to Ingres. It is something exact, conscientious, definite, all the lines perfectly clear—almost to the point of being dry. Hermant is a classic. And then, what a detail in costuming and manners! What intelligent snapshots—(with just a trace of irony) of current ideas, either platitudes or made to look like platitudes, but witty, witty—by the turn he gives them, and the setting! It is small-sized stuff, a little too small perhaps. He often reduces where he ought to enlarge. That is the only fault I could find with him. Nevertheless, he is a real master and a perfect writer. . ."

I always think of these words of Anatole France when I happen to be rereading, not the *Cavalier Miserey*, where Hermant is still under the influence of the Naturalistic school, just as France was in *Jocaste et la Chatte Maigre* (all the novelists of the period passed through that phase); nor yet *The Transatlantics*, where I find the gaiety a little vulgar; but rather the cycle of the *Courpière*, of the *Coutras*, along with *Les Renards* or *La Discorde*, and also the cycle which he called *Chroniques Anglaises*. For Hermant loves England and

"feels" Oxford in a very special way, almost as though
he were born there. On the psychology of present day
England—society and the academic world—he brings
home to France singularly exact and very amusing
observations which are superficial only in appearance:
in reality they strike very deep. In spite of his care
with "plot" and "suspense," and by virtue of his attention to the details of life in "society" and his interest in certain vices, which, if not new, are at least
more frankly talked about in our time, he is sometimes
regarded as a precursor of Proust.

This escape from Naturalism, characteristic of an
intermediary, a transition, period, is also visible in
Gaston Chérau (in *Champi-Tortu*), but with something
else besides: a sensitiveness as of raw nerves, something bitter and strong that lends a painful, almost
heroic, value to the pettiest details of that life of a
neglected child. It is the same in the *Prison de Verre*,
and in *Valentine Pacquault*, which are as relentless as a
novel by Julian Green, with, in addition, an instinct for
"doing things big."

In Octave Mirbeau (see his *Abbé Jules*) there is a
more violent sensibility and a stronger dose of exas-
perated pessimism, though these also are marked by
Naturalism, a Naturalism in which one detects the influence of the Goncourts, and even of the older

Romantic themes. In his *Jardin des Supplices*, an inverted satanic mysticism allows the heroine, for a second, to get back her baptismal innocence through the spectacle of cruel sufferings in others, and through the satisfaction, by virtue of a sex crime, of the desires that spectacle has aroused in her. A Baudelaire for chambermaids, one might call it (that is the title, for that matter, of one of Mirbeau's novels), but presented with a great, though somewhat loquacious and oratorical talent! Mirbeau is too often breaking in open doors which he alone insists on believing still closed.

There is Naturalism also in Paul Adam, who makes his début in *Chair Molle*, a mediocre book that tries to be inspired by the narrowest formulas of the school of Médan, then turns to Symbolism, and finally yields to the pressure of the Russians—especially Tolstoï's *War and Peace*. But on the whole, Paul Adam is steeped in Zola. Like Zola he creates a style for himself—a style that is Jack-of-all-trades and is applied rather wholesale to all sorts of duties. Like Zola he enjoys handling mass movements, and tries to ennoble the mob, as it were, lending to the convulsions of peoples, armies, countries, an "emotion of thought" in Tolstoï's manner. He too has his "idea-forces," which, later on, Sorel will more correctly call "idea-myths." They sweep everybody away and govern everything. *Le Trust* seeks to reveal the power of Money and the limitations of such power; his military and historical novels, *La Force, l'Enfant d'Austerlitz, La Bataille d'Uhde, Au Soleil de Juillet*, then *La Ville inconnue*, glorify leaders, conquerors of new lands, founders of colonies, masters of men who are famous for a second and die, while "the race" survives, the greater through their sacrifice—the only glory, the only immortality, is for the race! Paul Adam cherishes the dream of a sort of Latin imperialism. He was a vigorous personality and an intelligent writer, more intelligent perhaps than sensitive, but always admirable for his literary honesty and conscientiousness. The tears come to one's eyes at the thought of the almost sixty volumes on his list, of which nothing is now left except a fading memory!

But from all these examples it is evident that Paul Alexis, one of the most faithful bitter-enders of Zola's school, was not altogether wrong when he sent his famous telegram at the most critical moment of the quarrel between the Naturalists and the Symbolist reaction: "Naturalism not dead." The truth is that in literature as in many other spiritual domains, nothing ever dies entirely: literary schools replace, but also subsume, each other. So Naturalism succeeded the ideas of the "Parnassians," which had in turn succeeded Romanticism. So Symbolism took the lead over Naturalism. And I imagine it will be that way until the French language disappears—an event not likely to take place either tomorrow or day after tomorrow. Each of these "schools" retained something from its predecessors. And there are, and there will always be, subjects which will demand now Naturalistic, now Symbolistic, now Romantic, now Classic, treatment under forms apparently new. We need no better proof of this than the work of Lucien Descaves.

Sous-Offs., his first novel, dealt with the life of non-commissioned officers in the barracks, in peace times. It turned out something altogether "Naturalist." But when Descaves writes his *Philémon, vieux de la vieille* —so touching in earnestness and simplicity; when he devotes his refreshingly honest and straightforward talent to the good, solid "plain folks" of Paris; to the idealism of the old insurgents of the Commune; to everything in the "plain Frenchman" which spells real courage and a hopefulness as deeply ingrained as any inspired by religious faith, he does not need to change formulas: he simply introduces a certain note of dignity, of inward nobility, which comes to him, as it were, by nature. It is the realism of a "fine fellow," of a "non-com" with a heart, you might say.

Another descendant of Naturalism would be J. H. Rosny the elder. His *Bilateral*, while a very unusual and, at the same time, a very vigorous novel, is a document which contains a record not easily to be replaced of the state of mind, the political philosophy, of our first great Socialist dreamers during the early '80's. His style at that time still shows the influence of the Goncourts. Later on, his prodigious production grows prodigiously varied. Everything attracts him—he must know everything, and say everything. *Nell Horn* is one of the best French novels that have dealt with England in the Victorian era. . . . But there are Jews in the world! So he must know what contemporary Jews are like! And we get *Rachel et l'Amour.*

But above all—a rarer and rarer thing these days, Rosny has imagination, scientific imagination in particular. He foresees the remote future in the *Xipéhus* and in *La Mort de la Terre*, books of unusually ingenious inventiveness; and he looks back on the extreme prehistoric past in the astonishing *Vamireh* and the *Guerre du feu*. Next he turns to the fantastic, *La Force mystérieuse*, still in the domain of science. After reading one of Rosny's purely scientific works, *Le Pluralisme* (a novel of pure science, without "literature," without romance), a great physicist of our day, Jean Perrin (winner of a Nobel Prize), publicly declared that the elder Rosny was one of the greatest scientific philosophers of modern times. "Alas!" he mourned, "why did he ever take to writing novels? Otherwise we should have him in the Academy of Sciences!" But France is a country of "categories" and has been since Napoleon's time. In the eyes of recognized authorities Rosny is a "novel writer" and will never be more than an amateur in science. France looks down on amateurs disdainfully—just the opposite of England, where (I could give a score of examples!) a John Lubbock was first made a baronet and then a Peer of the Realm.

Rosny has often been compared to H. G. Wells, just as people have tried to identify Wells with Jules Verne —another mistake equally gross and equally ridiculous. Take all of the novels of Wells, in his first manner, one after the other! You will see that the scientific presumption, such as the fourth dimension in *The Time Machine*, or vivisection in *Dr. Moreau's Island*, is only the pretext and the starting point for a pamphlet in the style of Swift. In *The Time Machine*, Socialism has not succeeded. In a hundred thousand years, accordingly, the rich will have become just little fellows four feet high, passing their lives in playing prettily and in making love. They live on the proceeds of labor automatically performed by workingmen in the bowels of the earth. These workers, the Marlocks, have become mechanical brutes, unable to think; but if they cannot think, they can see in the dark! They come out at night to *devour the rich! Dr. Moreau's Island* is a biting criticism, you might say, of the Old and New Testaments. Dr. Moreau is the God of Genesis who lays down an arbitrary decalogue for the animals which he has changed into men, thus reducing them to slavery. Montgomery, his aid and successor, is Christ—but a Christ wrong-side-out, as it were. He says to the animals in question: "I was an animal at first as you were. I have come to reveal to you a doctrine of love!" The ethic of love does not work. Animal nature gets the upper hand again: and the animals try to devour their god!

In Rosny, on the other hand, the scientific fiction is the whole thing. It is self-sufficient and it fills out the novel without recourse to Socialistic or moralistic pamphleteering. It simply says: "This is what would happen if . . ." Nothing more—but nothing less! It is a case of a very learned scientist developing an hypothesis. There is nothing Swiftian, as there is in Wells, who has a much less extensive scientific background and is interested principally in social reform.

In a series of articles on the "Spirit of Modern Literature," published in the *Revue des Deux Mondes*,

M. André Berge asserts that our younger literary generation, coming around to a certain conception of the fantastic, where scientific super-reality would supply not only the pretext but the substance and the very form of expression in fiction, have been proclaiming their admiration for Jules Verne. They ought rather to look for their inspiration and their model to Rosny. He is an intelligence of the first order, and has not yet been given the recognition he deserves.

Henri de Régnier, in the same way, goes back not to Naturalism, by which he is not in the least affected, but to Symbolism—Symbolism, or rather a "free-verse" reaction against the regular prosody of French poetry, upon which the Parnassian school had imposed even more rigid rules. With Moréas, Régnier was the greatest protagonist of that reaction. Thirty years ago every last man of us could recite:

En allant vers la ville où l'on chante aux terrasses
Sous les arbres en fleurs comme des bouquets de fiancées,
Nous avons rencontré les filles de la plaine
Qui s'en allaient à perdre haleine.

. . . This free verse reaction played out almost at once. Two or three years, if that long, and Moréas was publishing his admirable *Stances*, and Régnier his delicate, scholarly, correct *Médailles d'argile*, meantime turning novelist and short-story writer, without ceasing

to be the poet he was above all else, and still remaining
a gentleman. Everyone should read such gems of perfection as *La Pécheresse, La Double Maîtresse, l'Amour
et le Plaisir*. Those at least are the books of Régnier
that I like best. The artist seems to be telling you:
"All this didn't really happen, you know. I'm just having my fun . . . but you—you must believe that it
happened! All voluptuousness has a savor of ashes.
Death, murder even, what are they? Come and sport
with me, beyond death, beyond time, like the fawn of
Mallarmé; for I am going to show you all these things,
not with a brutality that will make you shudder, but
with that supreme elegance without which there can
be no pleasure." Poetry is a great and a beautiful school
for a prose writer. He will never forget rhythm, measure, music. In Régnier these qualities are complicated
by a sort of detachment, half disdainful, half frivolous,
from the adventure he is developing. Often he seems to
be saying: "This is but a passing diversion; poetry
only is made for eternity." And there he is, straight-
away: nonchalant, eager, tragic, but ironically so; or
rather, with a sort of voluptuous superiority. He looks
preferably to the past for his subjects, at such times
creating a style which mingles the vigor of the Seventeenth century with the grace of the Eighteenth. He
revives libertines and sodomites who amuse without

shocking. He does not hide the fact that the ideals of his characters are ideals of self-indulgence. And one might say the same of his settings, alluring, sumptuous, smiling settings, something reminiscent of the Venice he loves so well. It is the work of an artist, and especially of a poet, who seems always to be saying: "You like this, do you not? But beyond all this is poetry—and poetry alone is eternal!" And then over these pictures which are so charming, even when fraught with tragedy, there broods, as it were, a higher melancholy which lends them a semblance of reality which Régnier himself, I dare say, would have been tempted to deny.

A poet likewise is Francis Jammes, a writer not to be classed with any school, unless we go back to Rousseau, Lamartine, Eugénie de Guérin. . . . He makes one think at times of a very good child able to find in the family library (down there in the Pyrenees) nothing but picture books, such as the *Magasin Pittoresque*, or the *Encouragements de la Jeunesse*, by M. de Bouilly —pictures that fascinated him as a child and came to life in his imagination, colored with his peculiar temperament of extreme sensitiveness—a sentimental sensitiveness, one of the rarest things in our day! It is through that sensitiveness and that sentiment and through those old prints and his mother's keepsakes, that he perceives people and landscapes. They become super-real, by dint of sheer unreality, from some little detail—the bells of a flock of sheep, the piping of a flute—of the real experience which suddenly acquires a delicate and deeply moving note of intenseness and truth. We can imagine our grandmothers saying of a book: "It caused me to shed very sweet tears." So it is with *Clara d'Ellebeuse*, and *Almaïde d'Étrémont*—the titles could not be better chosen! They take us back to a Romantic atmosphere long since vanished, which we vaguely mourn deep down in our hearts—they bring us very close to tears. Their style, like their sentiment, is "enchanting" in the sense in which the word was so often used in days gone by; one might say, the faint, but sweetly pure and crystalline tinkle of an old music box still perfectly in tune. There is something æthereal about it. They are not novels: they are exquisite romances of the kind that are written no more. Jammes profits by all that is divinely unusual in his nature. His conversion was sincere, I am sure; and I can imagine him being converted to recover the ingenuousness he yearns for, the childlike emotions of a "first communion"! . . . A woman writer, madly infatuated with her lover and knowing that she had botched her last book (she was a supremely intelligent woman), said to me one evening: "What do you expect! Happiness

does not go with my talent!" Jammes' ardent and naïve
faith, which seeks ingenuousness of expression above
all else, did not go with his talent. Perhaps only the
Madonna is to blame. She might have been more generous in benedictions toward her servant!

Jérôme and Jean Tharaud succeed in the unheard-of
feat of combining the documentation of the Naturalistic school with the style of Barrès. A scholarly, skillful
mosaic—too skillful, perhaps; and yet as substantial as
those so-called Roman (though more probably Hel-
lenic) mosaics which are now being unearthed from
the sands under the North African heath, as hard
and brilliant as the day when the artist-artisan put the
last touches to them! On close examination, documentation may seem to have a little the better of imagination.
Neither *La Fête Arabe*, nor the *Seigneurs de l'Atlas*,
nor the excellent *Ravaillac*, nor *Quand Israël était roi*
(not the best of their work) are novels: they are brilliant travel notes, or else luminous historical recon-
structions. In that case the Tharauds would be Vitet
(whose centenary should have been celebrated some
time ago), the Vitet of the *Barricades*, the *États de
Blois*, the *Mort de Henri III*—but a Vitet with infinitely
more talent than Vitet ever had.

But read *La Maîtresse servante*, which I prefer to the
two *Dingleys* and to the *Hobereaux*, slightly too remi-

niscent of Maupassant! Read especially a fine novel on the Jews of the European East, *À l'ombre de la Croix* (again perhaps a mosaic)! Zangwill's *Dreamers of the Ghetto* had already revealed the extraordinary activity and the will-power that is masked under the poverty of the Jews in Poland, Galicia and Hungary. But one of the Tharauds lived a long time in the latter country. He was able to see, and deeply to feel, the tenseness of that Jewish world. The novel, firmly textured and well-drawn, is a masterpiece.

René Boylesve, a native of Touraine, was as clever and as shrewd in getting along in society and in literature as Francis Jammes was not. The trait contributed greatly to his worldly successes, and somewhat less perhaps to his work, though the latter is far from negligible; for Boylesve cast a discerning eye on small-town society in France, particularly in the districts of Touraine. In their detail his novels remain trustworthy documents on the evolution of that provincial society from '90 on. There is more of the clinical spirit about him than the fashionable licentiousness of *La Leçon d'amour dans un parc* (in this sphere one has a right to prefer the work of Henri Régnier) would lead one to suppose. Though his manner is not strikingly original, he diagnoses carefully and soundly the symptoms of crisis and disease in the world in question. One may lament, perhaps, that entering a new world and frankly turning to society, the author of the *Médecin des dames du Néans*, of *Élise*, of *Mademoiselle Cloque*, did not have the courage to follow his bent to its logical extremes. To win great battles one must have a taste for risks!

Just such courage, and the sincerity that goes with it, are present in abundance in Édouard d'Estaunié, who may be lacking, on the other hand, in Boylesve's good humor—a smile that comes at times too easily and glows too readily for too many things. Olive Schreiner, the South African novelist, made a profound remark in this regard: "The external appearances of life are preferably amiable. It is the inner sense that is tragic!" Estaunié pursues this inner sense of things. He feels it from afar, divines it, is deeply engrossed with it. A mathematician from the Polytechnic, prepared by the Jesuits in the *Rue des Postes*, he did not deal gently with his teachers. Like Marcel Prévost in the *Scorpion*, he voiced his rebellion in his *Empreinte*, the very title of which "Stamped!" revealed the trends to which Estaunié's meditative, almost mystical, spirit will remain ever faithful. *Semel abbas, semper abbas*! His young man, a pupil of the Jesuits, will lose his faith, but will become a priest nevertheless: he has been "stamped," and the stamp carries with it a mission in life. The author does not say as much in the book; but does not Truth, in his eyes, mean that, when faith fails, spirituality remains? This, we may guess, is the conviction which has nourished and progressively exalted his talent. The mathematician is left a "spiritualist," and his spiritualism, perhaps in ratio with his scientific training, becomes more and more spiritualized till his whole universe is bathed in spirit. Spirit does not die: "Things *see*" says he—it is the title of one of his novels. They preserve again the "stamp" of events they have witnessed. The outward, everyday acts of men are nothing: hidden behind them is a real life, deep, unseen—their soul, in a word (*La vie secrète*). And finally, imagine some clerk in a public office, a man as much like that as possible, mediocre, painstaking, conscientious in his little tasks, thoroughly unimaginative; the love he will experience for a very pure woman who will not yield, who will never be his, will develop by degrees in him (*L'Ascension de M. Baslève*, Estaunié's best novel) a delicate spirituality, a sort of purified, sublimated, silent "ascent," without apparent goal, unless it be an imitation of the dead woman and her virtues; though she is not really dead: she continues living in him—and elsewhere too, we may be sure, on some other plane of the universe. . . A comprehensive and very exalted conception of the ethical life, suggested but never expressed, issues from this "spiritualism" everywhere latent. Estaunié's style is "proper," without artifice, without striking lines. Would not such preoccupations, in fact, signify irreverence toward the spiritual majesty of people and things? Emotion gushes, nevertheless, from an unobtrusive but intense earnestness. Estaunié's talent is very great—and a little sad.

I have just been considering a group of novelists, most of whom have very considerable and definite merits. Evidently they are quite different sorts of people. But all of them have one trait in common—a common destiny. In spite of their merits they have exercised no influence on the literary generations that followed them. Since the time of Barrès, the true masters, the real inspirers, have been André Gide and Proust.

XIX

WAR NOVELS

THEY can hardly be counted; several thousands at a low estimate! No end of talent went into them: such a formidable convulsion was calculated to supply genius to men, even, who had none at all. The war made clear that there is today only one religion with the right to claim a blood sacrifice: patriotism—if you wish, Nationalism. In days gone by the wars between Catholics and Protestants left such memories of horror, and such a sense of futility, that the thought of them could not have been without influence on a new principle which the Eighteenth century came formally to recognize: that no one should be put to death, nor even molested, by reason of religious faith. So now people are beginning to ask whether some limits should not be set to the effects produced by this new religion.

That is why the world quickly forgot, or tried to forget, the heroes who had told the story of the war in heroic fashion. At the most, *The Wooden Cross* of Raymond Dorgelés was spared. Imagine why! A battalion, decimated in battle, harassed, weary, dirty, wholly wretched, quickens step, braces its shoulders, as it enters a village, and a man cries: "Yes! Yes! We are the victors!" Another of these "heroes in spite of them-

selves" adds: "In that case, there will always be wars!"
And another supplies this tragically vivid definition:
"I call it a victory because I got out alive!"

Inadequate attention has been given to Alexandre
Arnoux's *Cabaret*, a collection of short stories, every
one of which is a masterpiece. This book is, to my
mind, the best work of this writer whose vigorous
philosophy, and whose exceptional power over words,
seem to have needed the terrible shock of war to bring
them to full yield.

Meantime, the immense and generous pity that filled
Duhamel's *Vie des Martyrs* and his *Civilisation*, the
shudder of disgust in his *Maquignons* and *Discipline*
—even the irony, at bottom despairing, of *Un Enterre-
ment* and *Le Cuirassier Cuvelier*, went to the heart, co-
incided with the impression the world had retained of
that ghastly unchaining of savagery. Duhamel was a
Major in the Medical Corps during the War. He had
seen too much suffering, he had seen too many die.
"Why? Why?" he cried. In this way this great writer
built up a personal religion, both mystical and stoical
at the same time. And he arrived at love of men for
themselves, even when they are gloomy and morose,
dispiriting. Whence his *Hommes abandonnés*! Whence
his type, Salavin—musings and dreams in a human
being who does not seem to have a right to muse and

dream; just a poor devil, as insignificant as millions of others; and yet, away down deep. . . . !

And before all this, in the full heat of war, in fact almost at the beginning of the War, had come *Le Feu*, by Henri Barbusse—the war in all its abomination and ferocity, all its dullness, filth, and vulgarity. And out of such material a book that is unquestionably great and powerful, a furious pamphlet which, in all probability, will live! It contains nothing new in literary method: it is Naturalism pure and simple. As I said a few pages back, certain techniques may seem outgrown or worn out, and the event proves that they are the only sound ones adapted to certain purposes. So with the Naturalistic technique of *Le Feu*, which was the only one conceivable for describing the War just as it was in the eyes of a squad of unfortunate, virtually nameless, men. So true is this that the writers who have tried to apply the style of Barrès to the same theme have generally failed. . . Nevertheless the Naturalistic technique has its defects. We must tell what a regiment is, what an army corps, what an army, what heavy artillery, what the quartermasters' corps. To do his interpreting Barbusse creates a character, Coton, called "The Cipher Man." And when the Cipher Man has recited, and finished reciting, page after page of the manual-of-arms, when he is of no further use, Barbusse kills him—which makes apparent how artificial the Naturalistic procedure may be.

On the other hand, Zola's influence is sometimes submerged in a Russian influence. And at such times a strange thing happens in the reader's mind. Barbusse pretends that a French soldier, a former miner, succeeds in crossing the German lines (a thing in itself implausible) and peering through a window in his house, sees his wife in the arms of a German. That strikes one as unreal, as falsely conceived. And yet, when we reflect: if we were reading that in Tolstoi or in Dostoiewski, it would seem to us perfectly plausible!

There is another curious thing. *Le Feu* is the first French novel, and perhaps remains the only one, in which certain obscene words are printed in full. The reason is that the army, in war time, was a world of men; and men converse with one another in just such terms. But there is, strangely enough, another reason: the censorship was in the hands of soldiers, and was wholly indifferent to such things. Its business was to prevent an author from revealing things that might injure the safety or the success of the armies. For commonplace decencies and proprieties of speech, the censor did not care at all.

And yet, even from the military point of view, such censorship was generous. It might have considered that to insist so strongly on examples of the misery and shame provided by a conflict which might have been portrayed in its heroic aspects, was harmful to the conduct of the War, to the "morale" of civilians and of combatants alike. So true is this that a German novel, "All Quiet on the Western Front" (*Nichts Neues im Westen*), which says all that *Le Feu* says in much more moderate terms, with much less lyricism, and, one must also say, with much less talent, was not allowed to appear until twelve years after the Treaty of Versailles! It took German literature all that time to produce "anti-war" books! In France such books appeared at once, and even during the War! It must be due to the individualism of the French! For that matter, it did not prevent them from holding Verdun singlehanded, and from winning the War, with the aid of their Allies.

XX

MARCEL PROUST

A DELIGHTFUL, spoiled child—delightful however spoiled; always ill and always supernaturally nimble in mind and even in body; a little prince from a fairy-tale who hardly seemed to be of this world—though worldly enough and perhaps too much so; born of the *bourgeoisie*, but a *bourgeoisie* almost too rich; of a mother who read Madame de Sévigné, and knew her *Letters* almost by heart; of a father, a famous physician, who had some Hebrew blood in his veins; gentle, but imperiously gentle, somehow managing to make every will bend before his—an ever-changing will save as regards writing and being a great writer; a little "catty" without meaning to be; eager as a woman is to please, and in fact pleasing everybody, but at the same time with the vainness of a child who, being an artist (many real artists never grow up), tries to make use of his winsomeness for the purposes of his art, flattering and cajoling with all the patience and ingenuity of a psychiatrist determined not to leave his patient until he has his notebook filled with points on a new case. . . . !

Proust was all this without trying to be, just by following his nature, perhaps perfecting and polishing it a little by frequenting the highly titled society of the Faubourg Saint-Germain, which knows the trick of hiding its utter indifference to those who are not "well-born" under a mask of delicately shaded courtesy.

His portrait? Proust sketched it himself, in the scene with the two nursemaids who are taking care of him in that mansion of Bolbec in Normandy, which was still fragrant with his memories of childhood, and "the shadows of young girls in flower."

"Oh, you little black devil with that black hair! Oh you wickedness of Satan! What could your mother have been thinking of when she made you? For you are just like a bird! Look, Marie, wouldn't you say he was preening his feathers and turning his neck—just like a bird? As light as a feather! You might say he had wings, and was trying to learn how to fly! Oh, lucky for you that those who made you had you born among the rich; else what would have become of you, wastrel that you are? Look, he's throwing away his roll, because it touched the bed. Well, well, better yet: he's spilling his milk! Wait until I put a bib on him . . . Oh, you never know how to manage! Was ever anyone as stupid and awkward as you? . . . Look at him, Marie! Bing! There he is, raising his head, straight up, like a snake —a snake, for all the world! . . ."

". . . According to her," Proust continues, "they

never knew when I did my sleeping. By night I was flitting about like a moth, and by day I was darting everywhere like a squirrel. 'But he doesn't like to have a bib put on him when he eats! It isn't that he doesn't like a bib, it's just to show that no one can cross him! He is a born big-wig, and he wants to show that he is! Ah, what a bag of tricks! How winsome, and what a cheat! Sly as ever they come! Rascal, rascal . . . !' "

And Celeste concludes: "Didn't you see, in your bureau-drawer, his photograph when he was a child? He tried to make us believe that they always dressed him very simply. And there he is with his little cane, a bunch of furs and laces, such as prince never had! But that is nothing to the way he carries himself: like a king! And with all that, a heart of gold!"

This is one of the best bits of Proust. Everything is there: the "princely" air, the capricious and enchanting wilfulness; the intellectual and physical agility; the need of being served, which results in a peculiar familiarity with servants; the insomnia; the unique gift for noting the most insignificant conversations, for showing people as they are—for posing them; and meantime for transposing conversations; for it is obvious that never did nursemaid speak in that fashion, though he notes that the brothers of these two women married, the one, the niece of the archbishop of Tours, the other, a relative of the bishop of Rodez (here again is another one of his vanities: all the people he meets must have something extraordinary about them).

And so—ill health from birth, though he survived till forty; some influence from his servants, whom he couldn't do without, especially the indispensable Françoise, who herself had a footman (the home was sumptuous, indeed); a sufferer from insomnia (well-known the almost hallucinatory enlargement of daytime memories that takes place during wakeful nights); son of a celebrated physician and himself accustomed, in the family atmosphere, to regard every word that was uttered as a clinical fact to be considered objectively; with a certainty that the smallest detail may be the most important, and that to know such details one must know how to "make people talk!" And what charm, what goodness—he calls the traits "adorable," himself —and he was in fact adorable: not only were the Jewish circles to which he belonged proud to point to such an attractive specimen of their race, but all his Gentile friends were infatuated with him. He added to a prodigious literary output an enormous, carefully worded, truly friendly or intimate, correspondence; and it was so flattering in tone that when he died, there came a whole series of "Tributes to Marcel Proust," "Reminiscences of Marcel Proust," "Letters of Marcel Proust," with annotations copious enough already to fill a library. One might wonder, at first glance, whether the author may not have had more friends than readers!

This doubt may be born most commonly of meanness and spleen. To be sure, writers are "launched" today much as patent medicines and new brands of cigarettes were launched years ago, and much as painters, actors and charlatans in general have been, and still are being, "launched." This may well be, but merchants (publishers) are not fools. They do not go in for large scale advertising until it is certain that their article "is taking," that there is a demand for it, a market for it. Proust had readers and he had admirers —hosts of them, long before any posthumous campaign for advertising. I remember, for example, the enthusiasm of the great, and great-hearted Rosny (the elder) at the time when *À l'ombre des jeunes filles en fleurs* came out. Rosny never cared a fig for the public and for publicity. Proust filled a demand at that time, and he had a market! He gave something new, a novelty that people had been expecting and calling for.

What was the "novelty"? One almost hesitates to state it, since within the limit of an essay such as this, it might seem in better taste to avoid remarks of a paradoxical aspect. But since we are speaking of the French Novel, the question arises, and cannot be avoided: is Proust entitled to mention here? Are his fifteen volumes (with the exception of *La Prisonnière*, which more or less will pass) really novels?

They are excellent, they are great, they are admirable "reporting" (reporting, with an emotional quality sublimated to the intellectual sphere, but nevertheless emotional) on present-day society. But what society? A society which, unfortunately, is restricted to a single class of people, the only class which no longer has any social importance, which is little more than a "witness," in the geological sense of the word, to a vanished era—imagine it, if you wish, as some gray and very heavy boulder left by the ice of the glacial period on a plain. It is a class that serves no purpose and does nothing: I refer to the French titled nobility, to the society, in a word, of the Faubourg Saint-Germain.

It seems to have been Bourget who let fall the remark that modern Europe "rests on three pillars: the French Academy, the English House of Lords and the German General Staff." Well, let's see! The French Academy is composed of thirty-eight or thirty-nine, rarely forty, very honorable and very justly honored celebrities. But I cannot see that it has exercised any great influence on developments in France: it is content to follow those developments historically, at very long range. One might say the same of the English House of Lords which is nothing more than a witness, a sur-vival, of eras long since completed. There is left the German General Staff: and the German General Staff led its country to ruin! Bourget, we are constrained to conclude, was not in luck. But was Proust's choice any more fortunate? The masters, the leaders of Occi-dental countries are, at the present writing, not our worn-out aristocracy of title, but—whether we like it or not—our politicians, our great bankers, our great merchants, our business men! Why did not Proust turn on these his exceptional gifts for observation?

Proust would have answered, tartly, that politicians and business men are not a "class" (or "classes"), but a "gang" (or "gangs")—and that such "gangs," once they become rich or powerful, have but one desire: to make their way into that useless society of titled butterflies; so great, even today, is its *prestige*! Or per-haps, speaking as a professional novelist, he might have given an answer that had been taught him at school: that it is among the useless and the great of the earth, among people who have time on their hands, who are not harassed and hampered by material tasks, who are situated above the common laws, that the play of passions reigns in its full purity.

But pray do not stop at such excuses, such "reasons." The truth might well be that for the charming Marcel, for this "scion of royalty" *à la* Gobineau (born what you please, but royalty for all of that, by virtue of the intrinsic and extrinsic qualities of his mind), to force an entrée into a world so exclusive, to be "received" in it, was, in itself, a conquest. Once there, why should he not "observe"—observe with the incomparable instrument he had forged for himself; observe what no one, since Saint-Simon, had been able either to see or to paint—save, it would seem, Stendhal, in *The Red and the Black*?

But just how far was the conqueror not conquered by his conquest? Certainly *Du Côté des Guermantes* is permeated throughout—one might almost say cunningly permeated—with irony toward that aristocracy he is so proud to frequent. At times his disdain breaks forth even more clearly: "There is, in the Faubourg Saint-Germain, such downright assininity . . ." And synonyms for "foolishness" or "stupidity" recur on several occasions in the same connection. At other times he goes hunting for excuses, justifications, which an artist would find legitimate: "In listening to the conversations between M. de Guermante and M. de Beauserfeuil on that subject" (genealogy and military precedences) "I was seeking only a poet's pleasure. And they, without being aware of it, gave me that pleasure, just as two farmers, or two sailors, might have done, discussing crops or tides—realities, I mean, too close to them for them, personally, to enjoy the beauty which I, personally, made it my business to extract from them." But, when all is said and done, he makes his excuses not only for himself, but also for aristocracy, even present-day aristocracy. In aristocracy he sees, not without due deference, "a heavy, ungainly structure pierced with few windows which admit but little light, evincing the same lack of airiness, but also the same blind and stolid power as Roman architecture, which encloses all history, walls it in, and scowls at it."

His aim was to seduce and reduce that society: he was, as could only happen, in a certain large measure seduced and reduced by it.

And half a volume to acquaint us with his as yet fruitless efforts to be received by the Duchesse de Guermantes! And the other half given over to the conversations, crocheted to the finest detail and most often (as was indeed his intention to show) detestably boring, in Mme. de Villeparisière's salon; to the old pun, already hoary with age when I was a boy at school, of "*Taquin* le Superbe" for "*Tarquin* le Superbe," which he makes the Duchess de Germantes repeat to satiety, *à propos* of M. de Charlus, and which, in turn, he makes all his circle repeat admiringly to his own satiety; to the idle gossipings of the pseudo-literary-and-musical salon of the Verdurins! Certainly we can credit Proust with the intent of irony in all that, but it is so long, so long, so long!

And yet he wanted it that way! Reread the interview he gave to the *Temps* at the time of the publication of *Du Côté de chez Swann* (Swann is himself; later on he will go over to the first person). . . . "Some young writers, with whom for that matter I am in sympathy, recommend a brief action, with few characters. That is not my conception of a novel. There is, you know, a plane geometry for two dimensions and a solid geometry for three dimensions. For me, the novel is not only two dimensional psychology, but three dimensional psychology—the other dimension is *time*. I have tried to isolate the invisible substance called time. But in order to do that, the experiment had to be of some duration. I hope that at the end of my book, some little social episode arising between people who, in the first volume, belong to very different worlds, will betray the fact that *time* has passed . . .

"Then again, just as a town, through which our train is following its circuitous track, appears now on our right, now on our left, so the different aspects under which the same person appears to the eyes of another person, to such an extent that he will seem several totally different people, will give, by that very fact alone, a sensation of the passage of time. One or another of my characters will be revealed later on as people quite different from what they are in the present volume . . . Isn't that the way it is in life?"

Proust goes on, next, to the importance, in a novel, of "unconscious memory." "As I see it, conscious memory, which is above all an affair of the intellect, gives us only false faces of the past. But how true it is that a perfume, a savor, recovered in totally different circumstances, suddenly reminds us in spite of ourselves how different the past in question was from what we thought we remembered of it; because our conscious memory, like a clumsy artist, had been painting it to us in unreal colors! Already in this first volume you will see the character who says 'I' and who is not I" (It was he! He had his reasons for denying it!) "suddenly remembers years and faces long forgotten, in the taste of a mouthful of tea into which a morsel of sponge cake had fallen. Undoubtedly he remembered those faces, those years; but without their color, without their charm!

". . . You see, only from unconscious memories should the artist draw the raw materials for his work. In the first place, precisely because they are unconscious, because they arise spontaneously, they alone (provoked

by the resemblances in an identical moment of time)
have a stamp of genuineness. Then again, they bring
things back to us in accurate dosages of memory and
forgetfulness. Whereas, lastly, names revive a sensation
under circumstances that are totally different, our unconscious memories free the sensation from all contin-
gency, give us its extra-temporal essence which is the
very content of style, that general and necessary truth
which the beauty of style translates.

"If I allow myself to reason in this way about my
book, it is because my book is in no sense a work of
reasoning; my feeling has supplied every iota of its
content, sensations which I first perceived deep down
in me, without understanding them, in fact experienc-
ing as much difficulty in converting them into something intelligible as—what shall I say?—as a musical
theme.

"Whatever we have not had to clarify ourselves,
whatever was clear before our time (for example, logical relations) are not truly ours, and we do not know
whether they are reality. They are merely 'possibles,'
among which, furthermore, we pick and choose quite
arbitrarily—as our style shows at once!

"Style is in no sense an embellishment, as some individuals think. It is not even a question of technique.
It is, as color is with painters, a quality of vision, the

revelation of the particular universe which each one of us sees, and which others do not see. *The pleasure an artist gives us is an acquaintance with one more universe.*"

A perfect and a magnificent definition! But what, then, of Proust's style? Is it, in truth, altogether the product of his memory? But it is impossible to decide whether his recollections are conscious or unconscious, since always, at all times, he seems to remember everything under the influence of sensations which are associated with one another and "recovered," as he has just explained in this interview, and as he will explain again, later on, in the admirable and celebrated passage at the end of *Le Temps retrouvé*. But is this always the case? That enchanting, magical intenseness of certain moments—does it figure in the two long passages in the last volume of *Sodom and Gomorrah* relating to "No. 40 *bis*, Boulevard Malesherbes"? Is there a blessed thing in either of those passages that means anything imaginable, that has anything to do with the subject of the novel, that has the slightest reason for having been written? Proust's memories, voluntary or involuntary as they may be, provide him with paragraphs of astounding power, things that are truly new, truly "unpublished"—I am thinking of certain impressions, tableaux, portraits, such as the passages on the death of his grandmother, on Albertine, on Saint Loup. But very, very often do we find a hundred, two hundred, a thousand, words too many; because everything is viewed on the same plane of importance. And, frankly, if the memory, be it voluntary or involuntary, is not worth while in any event, a style like that, so original in its way, and truly introducing us to an unknown universe, turns into gibberish.

Will you have an example? Proust desires to point out that the suppression of sound is not necessarily instantaneous. Yes—if one be deaf—there can be no doubt about it! A deaf person cannot hear milk boiling over! To perceive such a wonder in the world of the kitchen, one has to have eyes. Is the point conceded? Let's debate it no farther! But here is the way Proust puts it:

"A person who has become entirely deaf cannot even warm a bottle of milk without having to watch with all his eyes for the appearance, on the uncovered surface, of that white hyperboreal glint, as it were the threat of a snow storm, which is a warning that the wise will obey by breaking the electric contact, like the Lord calming the waters; for the spasmodically rising egg of boiling milk attains its climax in a few oblique bounds, swells, bellies out in a few tattered films on which the cream is creased, or darts another of mother-of-pearl into the tempest; all of which, if the electric blasts have been exorcised in time, the breaking of the current will set to turning over and over and drive to one side, changed into petals of a magnolia blossom."

What contortions, how much subtlety, for just nothing! One thinks of the euphuistic tirades in Shakespeare, which are always "cut" for the stage since no human being could listen to them.

So why then concern ourselves as to whether, perchance, Proust's fifteen volumes may not, as some have asserted, constitute one long immense novel; even if, in the course of that six-foot shelf of books, there be "preparations" so adequate that one devilishly clever critic was able to predict that two characters introduced in Volume I were going to get married along toward Volume VI or VII? Memories voluntary or involuntary weigh so disastrously upon this literature that the pleasure one seeks in fiction must not be sought in them. Novels? They are either "novelized memoirs," or "memoirized novels." You may take your choice!

The characters do change, change in attitudes and in temperaments, as time and these books go by. And that is what "often happens in life"—conceded! But the change takes place after so much, much talk, and such minute portraiture! Though there are amusing bits, now and again. Here is Madame Verdurin twitting Charlus, a man quite fussy about blood and family: "By the way, Charlus, can't you think of some ruined nobleman living out your way who would accept a post with me as my janitor?" "Yes, but I would not advise it. Many of your fashionable guests would never get past the vestibule!" Such scenes, such "talk," go on for so long, that when at last a character has "changed" you have forgotten what he was in the first place.

Yet, that is not quite so! You do remember one person—the Charlus just mentioned. Charlus stands all by himself in modern literature. In these "novelized memoirs" or "memoirized novels" Proust has built up a hero! A formidable and ignominious hero, human, realistic, an object of pity for his addiction to that sexual vice—call it sexual disease—which the world today is least ready to forgive; keen, intelligent, kind-hearted, at first secretive and sentimental in his viciousness, finally collapsing in public shame, in a painful, disgusting and abominable sadism! There you have the focus of the fifteen volumes! It is Charlus! Charlus has all the power and all the reality of a horrible type. He will live, for that reason.

XXI

ANDRÉ GIDE

IN HIS *Esprit de la Littérature Moderne*, M. André Berge, in an effort to find the kernel of Proust and Gide, makes a singularly apposite remark:

"By a strange paradox," he writes, "it happens that in all the volumes written in the 'search for lost days,' sensibility-emotion appears, at first sight, to hold an essential place. It is what first strikes the attention, by its originality and its acuteness. And nevertheless we are forced to conclude that the primacy remains with intellect: so far as the author is feeling, he is also trying to understand. What we really have is a marvelously perspicacious intelligence holding the stethoscope to a hypersensitized feeling. This is an intellectual tendency, but it is also a realistic tendency . . . Proust says, in fact, as though it were something too obvious to be debated: 'Art should be an exact reconstruction of life'.

"M. André Gide's tendency contrasts with this at every point: the fundamental primacy is held by feeling: but" (the "but" is mine) "intellect stands always in the foreground and in a striking manner . . . The center of his emotional interest is always a matter of ideas; but he considers them only when they are mixed with the feeling of some human being. In Gide, ideas are always incarnate in some character; and the characters are moved by ideas, whereas in Proust characters are moved by the feeling, the instinctive impulses, that arise from their ego. Here characters think, and they listen to the beat of their ideas as they listen to the beat of their hearts. They are able to spy on their own thoughts, and construct theories about themselves. . . .

". . . It follows that the lines of thought in Proust and Gide run in opposite directions. Proust starts with the particular and proceeds to the general" (here I am inclined to ask M. Berge whether he is quite sure that Proust always arrives) "whereas André Gide starts with the general and proceeds toward the particular, in the sense that going deeper and deeper into the human spirit—considering humanity at large—he ultimately reaches the individual soul."

May I try to say this in my own way? Whatever the extent of his sensitiveness (and it is great), Gide reacts at once. His first endeavor is to understand. And not until he has understood does he utilize his fundamental feelings. Proust has everywhere used, or claimed to use—I have said that in my opinion he does not always succeed—nothing but his involuntary memories. In Gide everything is voluntary at the inception of creation.

The result is that his work has a much wider compass, at least in appearance, than Proust's. It is not the human only that it strives to fathom, but the universe . . . I have before me the splendid volume that he brought back from his trip to the Congo and the Tchad. It is most interesting. In this book, the author of *Paludes, Isabella, Nourritures Terrestres*, the admirable *Symphonie Pastorale*, that *Porte étroite*, which is a masterpiece; *Les Caves du Vatican* so strangely—and somewhat heavily—fanciful; and *The Counterfeiters*, which I like not at all, comes forward as an explorer. He has all the perquisites of an explorer, one might say. His landscapes, while still descriptive in the literary sense, are "geologic," scientific. He knows botany and zoölogy. He examines the native in the perspective of the remarkable anthropological essays of Lévy-Brühl: *The Primitive Soul* and *The Primitive Mind.* In a word, he has the scientific spirit, and with all that, he is still human, and even humanitarian. Everything he says of the unpardonable mistakes committed in certain districts of the Congo as the result of the inevitable connivance between a few underpaid officials and agents of concessionary corporations, is true, entirely true. I would be proud to sign my name to pages like that! And I actually did something of the kind. twenty years ago, in Péguy's *Fortnightly Miscellany*, and no one had any reply to make! But nobody, so far as I know, has paid any attention to the wave of hypocrisy now radiating from Geneva. All foreigners claim the right to nose about in the colonial possessions of *other* nations, when the said possessions are not held in virtue of any "mandate." They are all dreaming of a redistribution of colonies; so that when a writer gives publicity to certain regrettable conditions, no matter how well substantiated, there is a general cry: "Keep quiet, for God's sake! You don't know the trouble you are going to cause us!" If, in spite of this, he is so imprudent as to write, his book is smothered under a ban of silence. That is what happened to Gide's *Congo-Tchad*, one of the best travel books published in our time. And I confess that what astonished me even more is that a wide-awake critic, like Paul Souday, did not perceive its singular merit . . .

But all this is parenthetical. The only question, in the literary sense, we have the right to ask just here, is why Gide turned to a subject which in no wise concerns him as a man of letters properly speaking. But the moment we dig down ever so slightly into his work we discover that it has, as it were, a trait of apostleship, of proselytism, due to his Protestant origins. This great writer, though entirely emancipated, has remained a Protestant not only in his besetting need of "converting" someone, but in the deeper and more inward nature of his astounding sensitiveness, and even of his intellect, which is always trying to master feeling and instinct and arrive at full understanding of them. He took his faith quite seriously at one time. He was proud of belonging to a religion which permitted, nay, commanded, a man to "make his choice." But when he comes to making his own choice he encounters an imperative injunction, on the part of the same faith, to go no farther. As a result—inhibition! Before Freud's time people said "constraint," and that meant absolutely the same thing. Therefore at the beginning of his intellectual and emotional life, inhibition and constraint of his most natural and imperious instincts! Nothing could be more painful for a boy or a young man who takes life seriously (and Gide takes everything seriously—that is where he differs from Proust); but in a literary sense nothing could be more productive. The more thought and feeling are obliged to react against the constraints laid upon them, the stronger the inner life becomes, the more original one's vision, and the more vigorous, the more violent, one's expression. But the violence remains, so to speak, internal. Imagine a man who is certain he must make the most impassioned revolt, but without lifting a finger. Would not the result be art? Gide said as much in a lecture on the drama which he published in *Nouveau Prétexte*. "Art is always the product of a constraint." That was not a confession: it was a profession of faith.

Witness the result in *La Porte Étroite*. I do not think there is, in all French literature, a more poignant novel. And how simple it is, at first! It begins a little languidly. One is led to expect a psychological idyll, something like Fromentin's *Dominique*. Two Protestant families! In each of them a young man and a young woman, lovers from childhood, with deep and desperate passions. There is nothing to hinder their marriages—nothing except a gloomy and sublime ideal of ascetism; one must learn to enter by the path that is straight and narrow—the path of renunciation—giving everything to God, taking nothing for oneself, controlling, restraining, refusing, happiness. And Alissa, the young girl, will refuse this happiness obstinately, ferociously. She will let her love grow to a sort of frenzy, to the most ardent, albeit the most chaste, passion, to the point where she sees objects, people, books, only through the man she loves. But she will do this only to control herself, to repress herself even unto death! One of her sisters also loves Jérôme. But in order to leave Jérôme to her sister, she will marry, without love, an honest, middle-aged man. Again that idea of constraint, but envisaged on another plane! She receives Jérôme more rarely. She adopts the recourse of Pascal: "Be ye idiots like the dumb brutes!" She gets rid of all the books given to her by the man she loves, and replaces them with pious idiocies. But she suffers, she suffers atrociously! That was what had to be. "O Lord," she writes in her diary, "preserve me from a happiness that I might attain too soon! Teach me to defer my happiness, and to find it again only in Thee!" And, farther along: "In despair of mastering my love in my cowardly heart, grant me, O Lord, the strength to teach him" ("him" is Jérôme) "to love me no longer . . . so that at the price of my merits, I may bring Thee his, which are infinitely preferable—and if today my soul sobs at losing him, may it be only to receive him later, in Thee."

And she tries to look older and to dress badly, that he may lose interest in her. And she tries not to write so beautifully, because beautiful writing is a vanity which might attract him. All this is torturing. This slow suicide—she ends by dying—is noted page by page, line by line. The diary could not be read aloud without stifling many a sob. But at last she dies. And this is her tragic cry: "Oh, of what use a virtue which my heart repels?"

And so, all this sublime, this superhuman and cruel

heroism comes to nothing! When Jérôme sees her sister, Juliette, again, married, a mother of four children, apparently happy, Juliette bursts into tears. Constraint, sacrifice, have not made her happy either!

Since the death of the old Romantic themes, a heroic and pathetic novel is one of the rarest things imaginable in French literature. And notice further that the theme of *La Porte Étroite* is exactly the same as in the *Princesse de Clèves*: the most difficult, and, consequently, the most beautiful achievement within reach of a woman is not to give herself to the man she loves. And, on the worldly plane, the result is the same: Alissa is unhappy, and brings nothing but unhappiness to others. Is there any difference as regards the *Princesse de Clèves*? The author of that old romance, in which God was not even named, tacitly glorifies this sacrifice to God. The author of *La Porte Étroite* will not be so clumsy as to say that he believes the sacrifice futile. He allows us to draw the conclusion for ourselves. At the same time, he informs us through his novel, and perhaps informs himself—that he has freed himself from his inhibition. Henceforward he will go on his way singing those lines of Emerson—which he has paraphrased, with a change of sense in his book:

> Space is large, vast and broad
> But two cannot go abroad.

Nevertheless, he will retain a constraint which he has banished from his conception of the moral life and from his relations with other human beings, in his manner, his style and his construction of a novel. His method is to choose, condense, coördinate. He is as closely compact in matter as Proust (quite gaily) is diffuse. He means to create characters, types. And in the book I have just described, he does create one, a most unusual one, as monstrous, if you wish, in virtue, as Proust's Charlus is in vice, and who lives as terribly as Charlus lives, but retaining our sympathies, which we cannot possibly keep for the supreme and blatant ignominies of Charlus which Proust does not hide, but rather displays with a certain fierce delight.

Gide was aware of this, and he said himself that "the supreme goal of art is to create character." And he added: "Every time morals are made freer, every time we get rid of an hypocrisy which forbids mention of certain things, Art is enabled to create a new character. How many Werthers-in-secret, who did not know themselves, waited only for Goethe's bullet to commit suicide?" Gide said that in 1904. Today we might add: How many Corydons, who did not know themselves, were waiting only for *Corydon* and *The Counterfeiters*, by André Gide, to commit "Corydonism"! Which all goes to prove, as I take it, that for people who were not caught young enough to begin "corydonizing," the theory has great possibilities.

Gide, with his well-known propensities for making converts, would probably answer: "Yes, why not?" Keeping strictly to the literary point of view, I would counter: "Because here your instinct for proselytizing has not served your talent. It has led you to the pedantry which Proust so admirably avoided; the pages where he treats in general of the vice of Charlus, and according to him of many other people, remain as clean-cut, as coldly objective, as the diagnosis of a psychiatrist. That, perhaps, is one of the cruelest and yet most substantial characteristics of Proust's work." But if I took the viewpoint of civic morality, I might answer that perhaps the progress of the Charlusian or Corydonian vice, or merely the literary publicity given to the vice, might well have some relation to the development to which I adverted some pages back—the progress of Malthusianism. The moment sexual instinct ceases to have reproduction of the species as its exclusive object, the manner in which people satisfy that instinct diminishes in importance.

. . . But on this point it might be better to consult some confessor of demonstrated competence both in morals and casuistry. I can go no farther, personally, on such a delicate matter, on which, nevertheless, I was obliged to drop just a word; for, surprising as it may seem, certain of the "Catholic" novelists of our time are inclined to some indulgence toward Corydonism!

XXII

THE CATHOLIC NOVELISTS

WE HAD them in France all through the Nineteenth century, that is to say, from the days of Romanticism; from the days of Chateaubriand's *Atala* and *Les Martyrs*. It would really seem as though faith had to lose its universal character as something imposed by force, as though it had to become a subject for free discussion, before literature could dare to consider it a proper source of materials. Add to this a certain process of reaction against the philosophical doctrines from which the Revolution had issued, an instinctive impulse to combat those doctrines and return to "tradition"! And what better, greater and more faithful guardian of tradition than the Church, unshakable, and, to all appearances, immovable in its dogmas and its moral teaching? And yet the *bourgeoisie*, and even a part of the aristocracy, had remained unbelievers, or merely deists, either after the fashion of Voltaire, or after the fashion of Rousseau—both were confusedly but potently mingled in many minds. It was quite clear, furthermore, that the Church, coming forward as the living prop of monarchical institutions, by no means intended to restrict its demands to the mere observance of its rites and a formal acceptance of dogma; but was setting up a form of surveillance over morals and private life which was accused of going as far as espionage; with the result that the Church became the bugaboo of all liberals.

But, while men were tossing Voltarian platitudes about and singing the songs of Béranger, they considered it quite natural, and (without admitting it to themselves) advantageous to their interests as fathers and husbands, that women should continue to receive a religious education. In any event nobody dreamed of secular education for women: they remained entirely in the hands of the Church; and this situation continued down to the time of the Third Republic. Now, people who read novels are for the most part women. Down to the end of the Eighteenth century men shared more or less the view of Voltaire: they considered, or at least claimed to consider, the novel as an inferior, frivolous and futile *genre*. Voltaire, to be sure, wrote *Candide* and the *Princesse de Babylone*, but to amuse Mme. du Châtelet. For women are not persuaded the way men are: if you do not use sentiment with them, you must at least be agreeable and light.

Balzac came out not only as a monarchist, but as a Catholic. I have already mentioned the very plausible explanation for this, given by one of the critics who seems best to know his work: before Balzac began to write, before he undertook his gigantic labors, he had lived his social life, his years of "freedom," in the aristocratic and political circles of the Restoration. Thereafter the institutions and the ideals which the Restoration pursued, continued to seem to him the best that had ever been. Barbey d'Aurevilly, as a matter of temperament, Villiers de l'Isle-Adam, idealistic, and of musical (Wagnerian) Romanticism, were also Catholic novelists.

And there was Huysmans! Here again reaction—reaction double and triple! A poor man, and an artist who passionately yearned for beauty and splendor, even tinsel splendor, Huysmans saw real, everyday life as abominably flat, wretched and empty. Equally empty, mediocre, banal, with its oratorical redundancies, was Romanticism! Equally empty, deliberately banal by its very technique, its grossly materialistic literary ideal, was Naturalism! He tried to escape them both in *À Rebours*, a childish but significant attempt to flee the platitudes of the real and the commonplace by recourse to the unreal, the artificial, the impossible . . . Imagine a child pretending that the cows in his Noah's Ark are real cows and that the real cows grazing in the meadow are made of wood! An amusing paradox, such as an artist would delight in, but wearing out after a few pages, and fooling no one, least of all the author!

Huysmans senses this, nay, understands it perfectly. Furthermore, this man in rebellion against Romanticism and Naturalism is, in spite of all, profoundly imbued with them both. Not their ideas, to be sure! But the superb "glistering," style of the Goncourts, the well-known style of Verlaine and Mallarmé—they were beautiful, in his eyes; and he set out to improve on them both. He is coruscating, staccato. He seeks the rare epithet, or the brutal epithet. And to the banality, the flatness, which he "feels" with unending disgust, but also with a sort of frenzied satisfaction, he will give relief and stress through sarcasm and insult.

There is also a touch of Baudelairism in Huysmans' case. Baudelaire may have been the one responsible for his taste for Satanism (in Là-Bas), and Satanism was the route to be followed to Catholicism. It was a Catholicism smelling of fire and stake, and, for all I know (I really don't care), it may have deserved the honor of the ban it received in the Index. It was a literary Catholicism along with (and in spite of) the railleries, inevitable in a man like Huysmans, against the "rats" (male and female) of the sacristies, against Pharisees and "Pharisettes" of all kinds, and against the sloppy sentimentalities of religious art in the Saint-

Sulpice section of Paris. But it was full of sympathy for this and that Christian, this and that priest. It was vibrant with eloquent enthusiasm for the architecture of our old Catholic sanctuaries in France, and the ideals they symbolized. What was Huysmans, in a word? A little man, crabbed and sour! His writing, sinning on the side of exaggeration, seems already out of date, doubtless because his main thought was of style. It tires by virtue of its straining for effects; but it is rich, nevertheless, in magnificent fury and in sincerity and dash. If it does not attain to religious faith, it strives to do so—a more interesting thing, perhaps, from the literary point of view!

Among the other Catholic novelists, or those with Catholic leanings—I shall not name them all, they are too many and almost all belong to the generations that are still young—there are orthodox Catholics and there are heretics.

The orthodox ones are the oldest in fame: René Bazin, and Henri Bordeaux.

It is the fashion today, even among young writers who pose as "conservatives," or rather as "Opposition," and who say, and perhaps believe, that they are Catholics (an understandable reaction against the scientific Positivism of their elders), to think of "poor René Bazin" with a sort of disdainful pity. They would all make of him a flat "hanger-on" of the Church vestries. I am not of that opinion. I am inclined to think these young men have not read him. And I hope I shall be credited with impartiality. I am not a partisan of any political or religious opinion, and this M. Bazin well knows. On the whole, we stand worlds apart. He shudders at the names of many authors whom I admire. I am sure M. Bazin, never departing in the slightest from his unfailing politeness, would think it a sin to say anything kind about me. But my position is this: I could never think of allowing any sympathy or antipathy in the domain of religion to interfere with a question of literary criticism. History shows me clearly enough that the particular attitude of any novelist toward the problems of the next world, and even toward political and social problems of this world, have no influence whatever on the impression they leave with posterity. What do we care today whether Stendhal was, or was not, an anticlerical; and Balzac, a monarchist and a Catholic? A writer avails by virtue of his power and his form, and the originality (so far as one is ever original) with which he expresses himself.

I do not know many paragraphs in all French fiction which emit the pure music, the ring of a crystal glass tapped with a silver blade, which one may find in the last pages of *Donatienne* and of the first hundred and fifty pages of *Isolée*. The most astonishing thing imaginable! Here is a man bound hand and foot by his beliefs; and yet you would say a George Sand clarified and condensed, a George Sand who had learned at last the necessity and the dignity of cadence and rhythm. But in Bazin, George Sand's sensuality is changed into pure sentiment. Catholic of Catholics among our Catholic novelists, he has the greatest courage! No theme more courageous (it borders on the shocking) than the one in *Isolée*. Bazin chooses a background among the laboring classes in Lyons for a young girl of exemplary piety, virtue, and Christian love. And how exquisitely, how delicately, he draws her! But she knows that her strength of character does not equal the fervor of her religious aspirations. She needs guidance, direction, a rule. So she enters a convent. There she is the holiest of the nuns. Comes the expulsion of the Congregations from France. The nuns are scattered. The little sister, so devoted to her duties, finds that her family has disappeared. She goes adrift and finally grounds as a derelict in a house of ill fame. She had no moral backbone—that was the cause of the tragedy: left to herself, she could not profit by freedom. When men afflicted with such mental and moral weakness cannot find a monastery, they turn to the Foreign Legion.

When women cannot find a convent, there is the house of prostitution!

I am obliged to admit that once the poor girl arrives in that horrible place, the novel becomes unreadable. People can write well only of the things they know. René Bazin was well acquainted with the mystical religious background of certain plebeian circles in Lyons. He was not acquainted with that other *milieu*, his pious feet never having trod such ground. There is no getting around it—the novel suffers from the author's virtue. It is none the less true that, if *Isolée* had been written by an anticlerical, everyone would have shouted scandal and sacrilege. This is why we may rightfully speak of Bazin's courage, and I could quote other examples —a scene (in another novel) between a husband and a wife concerning certain questions and procedures of birth control. Nothing would seem to require a more careful touch. Bazin is not careful. He rushes in, head down and double-fisted—his book reads like a string of sermons preached by some reformer of the Sixteenth century. So it comes about that the innocence of a great faith may bring a man to a recklessness which I am far from holding against René Bazin. Coming from him it is deeply moving.

And then come the non-orthodox, the heretics, and first in line the Manichæans; for not Jesus, but Mani, seems to have inspired *Sous le Soleil de Satan* by Bernanos. It is a remarkable work: one of the strongest and most vigorous that have appeared in recent years. It rings with a strange, furious, haughty music such as has not been heard since the days of Barbey d'Aurevilly. One is moved, shaken, rocked to the point of hallucination by the sombre and pious adventure of Abbé Donissan, whom the author has endowed with many of the traits of that miraculous and miracle working ascetic, the curé of Ars, who is now a saint of the Church. Donissan is a humble, timid, stammering priest, adjudged by his Bishop barely worthy of a charge in some rural parish; but he subjects himself to daily discipline, he fasts, he prays: he is a saint who heals the sick, a soul who knows no evil, transfigured by a beam of celestial light which seems never to depart from his person. And this saint, this austere worker of wonders, this incarnation of all virtues divine and human, is haunted by the Devil—at times by a devil in flesh and bones, the sinister figure of a procurer of vice! Donissan is beset by phantoms of impurity, and the struggle never relents. Despite his prayers and his austere penances he never feels certain that he has vanquished them and driven them away. Eventually he dies. Of the delirium of his last moments, the author writes as follows:

". . . The sound grows clearer. It is a prolonged, monotonous, inexorable murmur. He knows it well. There they are, one by one, men and women, all of them! He feels their breath rising about him, less foul than their foul words, dreary litanies of sin, words befouled by the ages . . . words passing from mouth to mouth, from generation to generation, like the pages of a lewd book which has been signed by Vice and countersigned in the prints of thousands and thousands of soiled fingers. The fog rises, and gradually envelops the saint of Lambres . . . And you can see those frightful children of iniquity, once they have caught breath again, groping with their lips for the hideous teat from which Satan will press forth for them the milk of their cherished poison. . . . 'Oh Thou Man on the Cross! Lift Thine hand in forgiveness and absolution, till Thou art dead! For Thou art vanquished before the battle!' "

Satan, in other words, is mightier than God. Evil will triumph over Good. Mani himself did not go as far as that! And you will even hear the Manichæan echo, somewhat attenuated perhaps, in *La Maison du Sage* and *Les Chiens de Dieu* of Louis Artus.

Now all this is very strange by virtue of a contrast which is worthy of note at a moment when the Church's teaching, sounding a prudent but perhaps necessary retreat, has been attenuating the absolute character of some of the Church dogmas, particularly on the point of Original Sin; and at a moment when neo-Thomism has been making such an interesting effort (inadequate and probably too long delayed, as M. Sartiaux points out) to reconcile reason and faith, Aristotle and Saint Augustine . . . It is very strange, and doubtless some reminiscence of Baudelaire may underlie it. But a Baudelaire badly comprehended: for M. Eugène Thébault has recently shown, in an ingenious and convincing essay published in the *Mercure de France*, that Baudelaire's Satan has a strange resemblance to the Satan in the *Summa*. It is not in the least impossible, for that matter, that the poet of *Fleurs du Mal*, who was fond of the Latin of the Middle Ages, should have read the *Summa*, or even have known it through one of those courses in religious education such as were given in his day in French high schools. Just what does Saint Thomas say?

"The evil angels," he says, "have a certain relationship with the good, as a consequence of what they have in common by nature. They even deserve great consideration, because there are things which exist and which the evil angels would like to see non-existent, and many which do not exist, which they would like to see exist."

What could these things be? Must they not be iniquities, imperfections in the Creation, human sorrows, evil in all its forms, ignorance? So that the Devil with his angels, in rebellion against God, becomes the interpreter of the anguish of mankind! Which puts quite a different face on him—a face, as we must courageously grant, no less menacing to the Faith. To be sure, Thomist theology knows how to get out of its hole, while utterly condemning the Manichæism of Bernanos!

Henry de Montherlant, for his part, could not be accused of Manichæism. He loves life too well. He wants it to be self-respecting, brave—and good. He would like the world in the future to live under a discipline something like the "training" of the athlete, something that governs soul and body in a sort of armored gentleness. And he declares himself (or at least did so at one time) a Catholic, but for the reason that he sees in Catholicism "the continuation of the Cæsarian idea." One may suspect that this definition would satisfy Mussolini more than His Holiness the Pope— not that Montherlant would care a snap of the fingers whom it pleased or displeased! He is sensuous, ardent, joyously following his youthful impulses as he claims the right to do. And his best book, *Gladiators* (a very fine novel which exalts the glory and the beauty of bull-fighting and the energy of those gladiators) ends

on a pagan note with an invocation "to the uncon-
quered sun"—*Soli invicto*, the god of the Roman
legion which camped at Heliopolis.

So Montherlant, one may fear, is not altogether a
restful recruit for the Church—any more than François
Mauriac is. To be sure, *Le Baiser du Lépreux* and
Quelques Cœurs Inquiets might pass as orthodox, making due allowances. But as for *La Preuve du Feu* and
Thérèse Desqueyroux and others of his books—well:
it is not that Mauriac lacks talent. He is chock full of
talent! Among the novelists of the younger generation,
he is one of the freshest and most profound, as witness
that same *Thérèse Desqueyroux*, or *Un Homme de
Lettres*, a splendid story fraught with poignant anguish.
But whenever his Catholicism crops out, one is inclined
to suspect that it does so to give greater relief, effica-
city, or, in any event, intensity to a riot of human passions, in all their most burning, sensuous and even
vicious forms. Mauriac too, at bottom, stands very close
to the Pagans.

Might I now venture a conclusion? For a century and
a quarter past the French novel has been flirting with
religious questions, but rare indeed are the novels that
are really "Catholic" in the orthodox sense of the word.

XXIII

THE NOVELISTS OF THE YOUNGER GENERATION

IN SPEAKING of Montherlant, Mauriac and Bernanos, I have already encroached on the domain of this chapter, and perhaps I should apologize for having introduced their work under that one of its aspects which is least pertinent to literature proper: the greater or lesser orthodoxy and sincerity of their Catholicism. Nevertheless, there is still room for a general view of our young contemporaries.

It is certain that the younger generation which has made its début since the War, in part made up of men who fought and in part of others born too late to enlist, stands before us already with a very considerable production. Publishers have never before issued so many books which are, or pretend to be, novels; though on closer inspection there are fewer real novels than one might suppose. It is also certain that this new generation of writers has come on the scene with new ideas and a new style of writing and composition (or non-composition, at least in the older sense of the word) and with new aims and ideals. Indeed, they deploy their well-manned cohorts before us (their ranks somewhat confusedly scattered, it is true) as

though bent on forcing through, in all branches of
literature and more especially in the novel, a revolution as important and as thoroughgoing as the Romantic revolution of a century or more ago (more, if it be
pushed back to its origins in Rousseau and Chateaubriand).

The revolution has been so marked that it is already
producing its reaction and its protest. While M. André
Berge struggles sympathetically to define the "Spirit
of Modern Literature," M. Julien Benda, in the *Trahi-
son des Clercs*, is vigorously arraigning our contemporary writers for playing false to the ideals of
disinterestedness and of generous humanism which exalted in dignity most of the great men who preceded
them throughout the course of our literary history;
and for being little else than advocates of certain parties
and certain theses, generally nationalistic and, in any
event, reactionary.

In other words, they are betraying the cause of the
independence and universality of Thought. More violently still in *La Mort de la Pensée bourgeoise*, a book
with the tone and the directness of a political pamphlet, Emmanuel Berl reproaches our younger generation
for what he calls its "conformism": its conformity,
that is, with the prejudices and interests of the French
bourgeoisie, to which it has basely sold itself. Our

bourgeoisie is alarmed! And it does not want to be alarmed! It does not want to hear about things calculated to disturb it! Our contemporary literature has therefore built up a philosophy, the purpose of which is to present things as so complicated that any change in them is hardly imaginable, and to pile up so many difficulties that people will despair of arriving at any conclusion. The aim is not to force a judgment but to provide excuses for adjourning judgment!

M. Berl thinks he can establish the facts as follows:

"The Orient, sprawled on its bags of rice, is looking for a morality. America is multiplying its steam radiators to the damage of all the historic values of the West. The whole world is tottering and the littérateurs of the world are not even aware that anything is going on. Imagining ourselves in the shoes of readers in the year 2000, and trying to reconstruct the France of 1928 under the guidance of our best works of literature, we would be astonished to see how little we could know. We would find no trace in them of the housing problem, and the financial crisis of the past five years."

The criticism, alas, is well founded. The French literature of our day is not "socially" minded: it is "psychological," and more and more so—how broadly, and how narrowly I shall try to determine a few pages hence. And yet, to evince an astonishment as great as

M. Berl's requires some ingenuousness. Our contemporary novelists are conformists? They adapt themselves too readily to the prejudices and ideals of the French *bourgeoisie*? But our novelists have always been and done that from the beginning of the Nineteenth century—indeed, they have been, all of them with rare exceptions, themselves *bourgeois* (calling his book *The Death of Bourgeois Thought*, Berl seems to concede as much). Flaubert, the great Flaubert, professedly a terrible *anti-bourgeois*, was nevertheless a great *bourgeois*. To be sure, he defined: "By '*bourgeois*' I mean everything that denotes low and cheap thinking." Which may mean anything you choose! But certainly it would be grossly insulting to our young writers to accuse them of thinking cheaply or vulgarly. Quite the contrary! They are concerned to think, or at least to write, "exceptionally." And many succeed in doing so.

Is not the fact, rather, that the French *bourgeoisie* has changed? It used to be liberal, and sympathized to some extent with the aspirations of the working classes; indeed, to such an extent that now it has taken fright, substituting the Communist scare-crow for the old Socialist scare-crow, which worked so well that long before the War not a few of our fat *bourgeois* began raising calves in their cellars and laying in stocks of canned goods in forethought against some "great night" of May-day! Now Emmanuel Berl is a Communist, and he dedicates his philippic to André Malraux, author of *The Conquerors* (a strong and noteworthy book, though a little too wordy), lauding to the skies the "labors" of those European Communists who were responsible for the attempt at a Communist revolution in China. Emmanuel Berl asks writers, born of our *bourgeoisie* and writing for our *bourgeoisie*, to begin doing books that will be, if not Communistic, at least "revolutionary!" Emmanuel Berl is asking too much! And, besides, I fail to see what our writers would be gaining, whether in terms of expression or thought, by doing so.

Not that there is any lack of a revolutionary freedom of expression and thought in France. We have such a thought and expression—only, it is confined to criticism and demolition! You can find it a-plenty in Emmanuel Berl! And as almost always happens to revolutionaries who have not yet conquered, and set up a *credo* just a little more narrow-minded than the one they destroyed, he mixes plenty of exaggeration and errors of judgment with several sound criticisms which he voices with furious violence. He says, with some semblance of truth, that our contemporary literature, our contemporary novel, has a cheap, ready-made, cut-and-dried conception of men and society; that it eschews strong and ardorous sentiments, and abominates ideas, "because ideas have an explosive force and threaten to disturb accepted conventions and the established order." A semblance of truth, I say: not the whole, or the real truth; for, otherwise, what are we to say of the patient, earnest and conscientious (also a little depressing) epic of *Les Thibault*, by Roger Martin du Gard? That our writers "detest passions, and particularly love, because love is rebellious to all discipline and would promptly bring rack and ruin to the world of marionettes they manufacture" is also apparently true; but only apparently. The reality is that "Love-without-danger" has become part and parcel of Occidental civilization through a weakening of family and marriage ties, through divorce, birth-control, and, in our great centers, by the progress of free unions which are tending to replace marriage, without the hypocrisies still prevalent in English-speaking countries, where divorces lead to remarriages, and remarriages to new divorces. All these pressures have combined to make love what it is, a pleasant and amusing game, which still proves interesting by virtue of ingenious psychological complications, but not by virtue of passion.

"The novelist does not love his characters," accuses Emmanuel Berl, further, "and he does not want us to love them. François Mauriac can do nothing but attractive boys who, unfortunately, are already lost, and pious women whom he admires but who are irremediably repulsive. Lacretelle is just as bad. And so is Julian Green! Rotting meat! Hearts and bodies grimy with mildew! Drunken, staggering, but *flaccid*, passions!" And he goes on: "Everywhere the revenge of the *bourgeoisie* on heroism! The modern novel is an empty valise which smells of mustiness from having been shut too long!"

A final condemnation, without appeal! At least M. Berl is not going to do any appealing! But that may not be enough for the rest of us. What pains me, in reading such pages, is to see so many truths over-stated or mixed with half-truths or non-truths. Berl's first mistake is of a general nature: he wants to make the *bourgeoisie* responsible for all the trouble, if trouble there be. And then—errors of detail! Is not Mauriac's *Fleuve de Feu*, like the *Lily of the Valley*, a novel of ardorous passion? Call it padded if you wish; but it is not more padded than Balzac's masterpiece, which makes slow reading, one has to admit. And how is it Berl fails to notice in Julian Green's *Adrienne Mesurat* a sort of austerity and fury that is *anti-bourgeois* and half-Protestant, at the same time, against that *bourgeoisie* that is Green's *bête noire*? Julian Green, an Anglo-Saxon who writes in French, a Catholic permeated with Protestant ways of looking at things, is, first of all, himself. But if he derives from anybody, he derives from Flaubert in *Madame Bovary* and the *Éducation sentimentale*! Berl is particularly unlucky in numbering Lacretelle among the defendants he drags to the bar of judgment. Lacretelle wrote *Bonifas*, perhaps the only "heroic" and "pathetic" novel to be found in the mass of our most recent literature.

Yet Berl's pamphlet is worth reading. Despite its extravagances and its errors it has its significance. But if one would have an antidote to Berl it is much more essential to read André Berge's *Esprit de la Littérature Moderne*. Not that Berge comes forward as advocate-defender. He substitutes explanation and interpretation for recrimination. He helps one to understand what is going on in France at present. It is all of the greatest interest! It would be unfair to attempt a summary of it. I shall simply borrow a few of the leading ideas.

Our newer novelists are not what they are because of any "conformism" or conformity with bourgeois prejudices. Their trouble is "psychology!" They are "psychologists," continuators of a tradition that has very remote French origins, going back at least to Stendhal and perhaps to the *Princesse de Clèves*, and whose nearer precedents may be sought in Barrès, Proust and Gide. While scientific psychology, despite the influence

of Bergson, has turned into psycho-physiology and
therefore remained Positivistic, our novelists, following
the lead of the masters mentioned, have adopted the
procedure of "introspection." This new introspection
has nothing to do with the old-fashioned "psychology
of the spirit." It is something quite the opposite. Intelligence serves only as a tool for discovering, in minutest
detail, the stirrings and impulses of sensation and feeling. These young men are more or less intellectualists,
or more or less "sensitive"—they are realists in a more
comprehensive sense of the word: "the function of Art,"
says Proust, "is to reconstruct reality." In any event,
closely observing themselves, noting sensations, whims,
worries, fears, they try to reproduce what is "elementary" in their psychic processes which are themselves reduced to equally elementary forms, and with
special stress laid on "contradictions." That is why, as
Berge says, "their characters seem to be tossed about
helter-skelter by events in which they seem able to find
no meaning. They lack any moral concept around which
a personality might crystallize. So they seem now 'un-
certain' " (in the work of Maurice Betz), "now 'empty
valises' " (in Drieu de la Rochelle, who began as a
poet, and has remained a novelist and a short-story
writer despite his fame as a political philosopher),
"now 'lost bodies' " (in Philippe Soupault—such a

brilliant and interesting man to follow!). We might note, in passing, that the title of "empty valise" which La Rochelle gives to one of his novels, is the epithet that Berl in his arraignment hurls at all contemporary literature.

And in all this we have something not a little bewildering; and it contributes without a doubt to alienating certain kinds of readers, who happen to constitute the largest market for fiction. These things are not novels: they are, so to speak, psychological poems in prose, and the poetry is wholly subjective. André Berge rightfully cautions that when the author happens to know how to tell a story, when he is a skilled craftsman (as is the case with Emmanuel Bove, Pierre Bost, and some others) "interest" still survives, since the writer is able to create an illusion of reality in any event. The point is well taken; but the "reality" is none the less draped in a kind of fog, an atmosphere of brooding sadness.

Most of these youngsters claim descent from the Russians, especially from Dostoiewsky. But there is one difference between the Russian procedure and theirs. Our young Frenchmen see themselves in the rest of mankind, or in a few people (when, as is not always the case, they know anybody). Introspection always lies at the base of their method. The great Russians, on the contrary, saw others through themselves—they were interested in the acts, and the contradictory impulses of others. They disappear completely behind, or in, their characters and the struggles of their characters. Whereas, how many of our more recent novels begin and end with the pronoun "I"—the unavoidable consequence of the literary method of introspection? Along with Gide our young men are declaring that one of the qualities which they esteem most highly in a literary sense is sincerity. But it is sincerity as regards themselves, and the sincerity is not extended to others—to what is "non-ego," in the same measure. Everything goes on inside themselves. Many of our present-day novels are psychological autobiographies, with a minimum of external events, a minimum of everything that made up a "subject," and constituted "romantic interest" in our novels of other days. Now the fact is, after all, that humanity at large, even humanity represented by its best and most cultivated brains, is not so different from "Jenny the Working-Girl," who breathlessly opens to her continued story in the newspaper each morning to find out "what is going to happen next."

And the old gaiety is gone, giving way to a sort of cocasserie. The latter appears, to be sure in an ultrasuperior form, in Proust himself. Having sharpened his observation of his own ego to a fine edge, living wholly within himself, he is inclined to see in the lives of others only an absurd dream. Then, at moments, he wakens from the dream, still half remembering it: he finds it still more absurd. And he says so. For that matter, the rate of speed at which people are living today enables us to see things only in a sequence of abrupt shocks, without having time really to understand them. Jazz and the moving picture act in the same way. It is a jump from sensation to sensation, with no leisure for the reasoning that explains and interprets, or for a gentle good-natured scepticism. "The whole campaign against Anatole France, since his death," writes André Berge, "is much more a campaign against an intelligence and a mood that are out-of-date than against the writer himself. But this new kind of wit, or rather humor," he adds, "all ends in a sort of uneasiness, or in despair."

Whence arises this sadness which is now so generally being felt, even when unexpressed, and which is radically different, when expressed, from the despair of the early Romanticists? In large part, without doubt, from the effort exerted since the Goncourts, since Naturalism, and since Barrès, and with a regularity that reminds one of the slow foldings of the earth's crust to which the geologist points, to separate sensitiveness from sentiment, and emotion from sentimentality. In this regard, our contemporary intellectualism is probably more positivistic than it would wish to be—a result one would naturally expect from the profoundly psychological tendencies of our literature from its very beginnings, and also as a very legitimate reaction against the debauch of sentiment in which the Romanticists indulged. But the fact helps to explain why such a remarkable novel as *Nono* by Gaston Roupnel failed of recognition even from our best critics and has never been accorded the distinction it deserves. Nono is a drunkard and a wanton, magnificent and wretched—he does right, he does wrong, he laughs, and he weeps. He is a man from Burgundy, and he acts like a Russian peasant! Roupnel's novel is perhaps the closest approach to the Russian manner that we have in French, though the author surely never dreamed of imitating anybody. But he is "sentimental," and in that he was running counter to the whole momentum of our literature (the point was called to his attention at the time!).

Another consequence of this crushing of the sentimental under the purely sensitive, and of this tyranny of the introspective method, has been a more and more complete vanishing of the character, the type, and therewith, of the heroic, in our novel. Not one of the characters in contemporary fiction stands out in such relief in our memories that we can say of a man or woman we might meet in real life, what we might say of the older types: "He is a Fabrice," or "a Julien Sorel"; or "She is an Emma Bovary." Nor can one think, over the fifteen years past, of a character in the slightest degree heroic, with one possible exception (along with Proust's Charlus), which must be credited to Lacretelle.

If, in a word, one would be satisfied with a rapid glance at the French fiction of our time, one would be tempted to define it as a series of little laboratories devoted to psychological micrography. These laboratories exchange their "discoveries," and boast of them not only as "new," which they often are, but also as "important," which is not so easy to concede. Our young men are calling a "novel" something that is half, or at least not the whole, of a novel. There has never been a greater dearth of real novels than at this time when the production of fiction is truly staggering. But it is a matter of autobiography, or of travel diaries (like Durtain's *Hollywood*—Durtain is a man of talent); or of amusing buffooneries (like Jules Romain's *Copains*), which sport preferably with the implausible or the impossible; or even of simple notes on realities more or less transformed (Proust, but with even less cohesion than Proust) by inconsequential contacts and slender reflections of characters. Sometimes, indeed, the characters are invisible, or at least undiscoverable.

Before this fiction of our day one may well stand as bewildered as the loyalists of Classicism stood before the Romantic revolution of the early Nineteenth century. The fact is that we are witnessing at present a reaction of much greater scope than that of Naturalism against Romanticism, or of Symbolism against Naturalism. Symbolism and Naturalism were deeply imbued with Romanticism. The literature of our time is infinitely less so. It is almost purely intellectualist.

And since this new literature, in large part introspective, has been spading a new field, it has needed a new spade, in other words, an instrument, a style, adapted to new requirements. It has fashioned one for itself. The elements it borrowed from Barrès, from Proust, from Gide; but the thing as a whole is its own, and it is something very personal. This new style, like all beginnings, has had its exaggerations, and its mistakes; but it also shows new and original qualities. May we not measure the intensity of a literary current by the importance of the modifications it introduces into style? The "sentiment of Nature," for example, was discovered about 1720, and an effort was made to remodel and revive French letters around that sentiment. The effort was a failure because the only language, the only style, available, was the abstract intellectual language of our great Seventeenth century Classicists. The tool would not work: the edge crumpled at the first strain! We had to wait for Rousseau.

Now, the creators of a new style are unquestionably deserving of renown and glory as inventors. If these young men have invented a style, it is because they had something to say that could not be said in any other way. Take the case of Jean Giraudoux: facets— images provoked by association, with the second term of the association omitted, as in the poetry of Rimbaud! *Suzanne et le Pacifique* is an excellent example of the interest and the amusement (as well perhaps as the irritation) this manner may arouse in a reader. You can find another specimen in *Siegfried et le Limousin*—and that iridescent, mottled surface, amusing, sparkling, runs the risk of being anything you may choose to call it. But then *Siegfried et le Limousin* is put on the stage in dramatic form. For the theatre, the language has to be clarified, condensed, reduced to more everyday terms: and the passionate drama comes to life, the conflict between the two antithetical races, the two antithetical aspirations, of modern Germany! Under such stylistic novelties, an idea, an intelligent deep-piercing idea, lurked! And would the author have

been able to express it without those innovations? . . .
Wherefore it occurs to me, as an acceptable hypothesis,
that while the stylistic budding season at present in
progress may not be all one might hope for in the
novel, it may do something for the stage . . . and
the stage in its turn may . . . who can be sure?

But even now, and in the domain of the novel alone,
we have Jean Cocteau. It is a very curious thing! Guil-
laume Apollinaire may perhaps have had an influence
on his talent, for Apollinaire was one of those inventors
of style and of entirely new literary procedures of which
we have just been speaking. In Cocteau, accordingly,
we have rogueries and tomfooleries and then, all of a
sudden, melancholy poems of an exquisite classic purity
—romance, in other words. Take one of his latest, *Les
Enfants Terribles*. Methods utterly unexpected, created,
so to speak, in order to drag the reader from what he
knows by experience to what he has never experienced
or seen—to another world! The thing begins with an
exact, living, sharply drawn, truly Balzacian picture
of "Monthiers Alley," where the little shavers of the
lower classes of the Lycée Condorcet are settling their
little differences in individual combats; and a picture
of those youngsters themselves—thoroughly up to the
minute in their clothes and in their tastes (moving-
picture halls, the prize-ring, jazz, girls), but eternal in

their essence. And then suddenly one of those boys and his sister, at first semi-orphans, then orphans! And here it is that we enter the non-seen, the non-known, the new, the unexpressible (but expressed) disorder of a child's Bohemia, an utter lack of knowledge (indeed that of children and very young people) of the real life and the real outer world, of which their only notions have come from books (often shocking books "beyond their years"), from absurd illustrations and memories of motion-picture plays equally far from reality. This brother and this sister insult each other constantly; they quarrel, they fight; and they do so, understanding (the lucid intuition of the adolescent mind) *that it is all in fun*; whereas the *others*, all the rest of their friends and acquaintances, take their fun for reality. Hence a notion of their superiority over those *others*, because of the stupid mistake those others are making. And hence also an inextinguishable passion for that fun, even when they are grown up and are man and woman; and therefore a radical incompatibility of their lives with the lives of others by virtue of the fun they still continue. They are "a world" to themselves. And therefore, hovering over both of them, incest . . . an incest that will never be consummated, but which dominates them and controls them. . . There will come a young girl who does not understand their game, since it is not explained to her. She, of course, will fall in love with the brother. The sister, jealous without realizing it, will persuade the brother, who is enamoured of the newcomer, that the latter is in love, not with him, but with a friend of his. The girl will marry the friend. And, when the deception is discovered, the brother will poison himself, with a "negro" poison. . . It is this latter part that spoils the book. This "negro" business has heretofore not been prepared for, or at least, unskillfully prepared. The marriage, or marriages (there are several) and what happens afterward, are treated in a slovenly manner. This novel, which might have been a great novel, something definitive, finished, absolute, dwindles to the proportions of a truncated short story; or rather, the beginning is that of a great novel; the ending is neglected, sacrificed, by a sort of indifference. And yet, the book closed, you will have the impression that you have never in your life "read anything just like that."

There is Paul Morand, in whom we find no trace of introspection, but direct observation of the world and of human beings, viewed whimsically and cynically; but along with that, a technique of style and consequently a manner of presenting images closely related to Giraudoux's, a subtle and original teacher, one must confess. Morand is "sensitive," though it would seem that being amusing bores him. Morand is extraordinarily intelligent. He can do better than that! An article signed by him in the *Nouvelles Littéraires* explains the mood of indifference to which he has been brought by his researches in style. So he turns traveller on "nothing but the earth," which seems to him a very trifling affair; and now he has a direct, meditated vision of things, with an afterthought that is half political, half practical —but at any rate original. In Morand, plain intelligence has taken the lead over intellectualism, at the expense of fictional inventiveness. This for the moment! If ever he gets back to the novel, what may he not do!

And finally we come to Lacretelle's *Bonifas*. It is something literally extraordinary, one of the strongest, the most "pathetic" things perhaps that has appeared for a long time; and it is related, not to Stendhal, but to the work of Balzac, of which it is quite worthy! And if, so far, it has not been given its rightful place, is it not because it shuns (properly, necessarily) similarities, analogies, with other productions of the present time, down from the time of Proust and Gide? As is the case, in a certain number, at least, of those works, there is a leading character who has whims for a devouring and besetting passion that is in itself disgraceful and an abomination in the eyes of the public:

Bonifas is a woman without grace, without beauty. She looks like a man. Born and growing up in a small country town, she feels her impulses irresistibly sweeping her toward the sex to which, by a mistake of Nature, she belongs. Do not wince just yet: in *The Girl with Yellow Eyes*, and *A Passion in the Desert*, and other novels still, Balzac went much, much farther! Bonifas does not yield to this hankering, she dares not yield to it: she smothers it! It turns to sentiment; to sentimentality (could there be any worse crime, according to present day literary principles?). She all but adopts a poor working-girl who is suffering from tuberculosis. She takes her to the South of France and helps her to die in some comfort. She remains meanwhile, and in every respect, *virgo intacta*, but no one in her little town believes so, because of the eccentricity which her "repression" lends to her manner. As a result, slanderous gossip, obscene songs! She immures herself in her house, emerging only for long horseback rides, by which, as she grows older, she tries to kill the demon that still dwells within her. . . Comes August, 1914! On one of her rides she sees the first German Uhlans approaching. She dashes home at a gallop, spreads the alarm! Terror and cowardice on all hands! It is now that *the man* in her, the virility which her unfortunate feminine body has so long restrained, explodes. Bonifas takes over the government of the town. She it is who wrestles with the Germans for four long years. The War over, triumph, deification, decorations, receptions of honor, toasts by celebrities! And at one of these meetings, at a young girls' high school, as she stands before young maidens who have been brought up as she never was, and who will never know the torments she has known, she bursts into tears . . . The history of the War records a case of a woman who did, in a small town in France, exactly what Bonifas did (in the second part of the novel, I mean, not the first!).

So stern are the laws of our new literary technique that a critic, and by no means one of our lesser ones, concluded, at the time this novel appeared, that it was noteworthy in the first half, but only passable in the second. Once again damnation of heroism! While significant as to present-day tendencies, it is enough to make one laugh!

In the first part there is some padding. In the second there is none. All that one might regret, it seems to me, is that Jacques de Lacretelle has not yet given us a sequel to *Bonifas*. One volume is not enough to make a Balzac. But he gives the impression that he could be one.

Let us therefore take this novel only as proof of a

very simple literary law. No literary revolution, any more than a political revolution, can succeed save on condition that it absorb at least a part of what has preceded it and adds something thereto. That is true even of Romanticism—we have full proof of it at present. Whether we like it or not, the good novel will always have about it something of the epic which, in the last analysis, gave birth to it. It must be living, heroic, or comic, like the *Chanson de Roland* or *Don Quixote*, but at any rate living in its action. Its characters must seem to be alive: they must be, as far as possible, types representing more or less universal characters; or else, on the other hand, monstrous exceptions, such as Proust's Charlus, who, when all is said and done, is a sort of realistic Manfred, a Manfred stripped of his Byronism. Otherwise, the novel is not a novel. It may be something infinitely interesting, even a masterpiece, like Proust's work; but it is something else. Nevertheless, we see that, all the way along from Gide's *La Porte Étroite* to Lacretelle's *Bonifas*, there have been real novels, fine novels. And, finally, the new tool, that is to say the new style, has been created, or at least suggested, for doing something new in the novel. The fact is of capital importance. The only problem now is to use it to produce more often a more human work of general interest; and that far Julien Benda and Emmanuel Berl are right!

I was about to forget: the new literary generation said: "Science, the application of science to human life, and what might be termed the new metaphysics derived from the latest inferences from science, have changed everything in the world." That is the exterior truth of which we must take as liberal account as possible. But the inner and supreme truth is, that the novel, above all, is men and women, eternal in their ever changeless passions, living under changed conditions and reacting one upon the other. In contemporary literature this is not always the case: our writers tend to think only of themselves and to react only upon themselves.

And here I was about to close but I find that I have one thing more to say: May it not be the fault of the new literary method of introspection that the social novel—by that I mean the novel of political and social observation, as in Balzac, and Stendhal, Zola, and even Barrès (in *Les Déracinés*)—is so rare today? And nevertheless almost all our young writers, repudiating Art for Art's sake, declare that they have one political opinion or another! Now, at the present time, there is not a single novel in which an author has tried to reconstruct French society between 1870 and 1914! Yet it is a subject worthy of some attention. . . One thing is clear: little men, very little men without any distinction, men forgotten almost as soon as they die or fail of reelection, lay hold on the government of France during that period. They seem low and vulgar enough in the external manifestations of their personal ambitions; because, under a parliamentary system, the means of attaining power are always low and vulgar. And yet, from the political and social points of view, they accomplish gigantic feats: they democratize and secularize France! They introduce a radical transformation in the education of women! Patriots, in spite of everything they obtain after all better results than the earlier governments, since the régime they serve (and plunder) has managed to survive, while its military and diplomatic competence has been great enough to win a war that the preceding régime had lost! Here, then is the question:

How did this period between 1870 and 1914 come to produce the France we have today, with all her qualities and defects, her possibilities and her anxieties? The theme would have tempted Balzac, were he alive today. He would have shown us a number of more or less attractive fossils, a number of reckless adventurers, a number of fairly decent people doing some fairly rascally things, a number of mediocrities, and, I imagine, degenerates doing some great things. That is what Balzac did for an age when France had just emerged under new aspects from a series of formidable wars, and a formidable Revolution . . . In our day this great theme has been barely touched in the "Bergeret" cycle by that Anatole France whom the younger literary generation would disdainfully push down into a Hades of forgetfulness; in the subtle annotations of Abel Hermant on Parisian society; in the extraordinarily acute work of Marcel Proust, which, however, taken as a whole, bears almost altogether on the most insignificant and ineffective of our social classes (Proust shows that very thing, for that matter), a moribund, mummified aristocracy; and finally, in *Les Thibault* of Martin du Gard.

In the perspective of this after-the-war period, might there not be matter for a new Balzac? But no one seems to have it in mind. Is it the fault of our present day formula for the psychological, introspective novel? Or has our creative imagination dried up? Or do the two causes combine? . . .

THE END